Abuse of the Elderly: Issues and Annotated Bibliography

Abuse of the Elderly

Issues and Annotated Bibliography

compiled and edited by
Benjamin Schlesinger and
Rachel Schlesinger

University of Toronto Press
Toronto   Buffalo   London

© University of Toronto Press
Toronto   Buffalo   London
Printed in Canada
ISBN 0-8020-6694-1

Canadian Cataloguing in Publication Data

Main entry under title:
Abuse of the Elderly
Bibliography p.
Includes index.
ISBN 0-8020-6694-1
1. Aged – Canada – Abuse of. 2. Aged – United
States – Abuse of. 3. Aged – Canada – Abuse of –
Bibliography. 4. Aged United States – Abuse of –
Bibliography. I. Schlesinger, Benjamin, 1928-   .
II. Schlesinger, Rachel, 1936-   .
HV1451.A36 1988   362.8'8'0880565   C88-093323-2

CONTENTS

vii Contents

PREFACE

This source book on abuse of the elderly, attempts to focus on this topic, which emerged a decade ago in North America. The ten essays written by professionals from the medical, nursing, psychiatric, social work and social sciences fields summarize the up-to-date knowledge of abuse of the elderly.

The Annotated Bibliography contains 267 items from American and Canadian sources. The entries date from the 1978-1987 (August) period, and are divided into 43 categories for easier reference. The appendix contains the addresses of most of the citations, in case the reader is interested in obtaining copies of the specific notation.

The resource section contains a list of research studies, a basic library on abuse of the elderly, and visual aids available on the topic with appropriate addresses.

We hope that this volume will help students, teachers, concerned professionals as well as the public to obtain a basic understanding of this emerging aspect of family violence.

ACKNOWLEDGMENTS

We would like to thank the following persons for helping us to produce this book.

Shayna Adelberg, Toronto Mayor's Committee on Aging; Cyril Greenland; Madeleine Grant, former librarian of the J.W. Crane Memorial Library; Jill Patrick of the Programme in Gerontology at the University of Toronto; Mary Parthun, doctoral candidate; Elizabeth Podnieks of the Faculty of Nursing Ryerson Polytechnical Institute; Blossom Wigdor Director of the Programme in Gerontology at the University of Toronto; and the Clearinghouse on Family Violence, Health and Welfare Canada.

R.I.K. Davidson, our editor at the University of Toronto Press and Virgil Duff, the managing editor of the University of Toronto Press, guided our writing.

We are especially grateful to the Laidlaw Foundation of Toronto, whose Executive Administrator Nathan Gilbert helped us to obtain a small grant to produce this book. Our family consisting of our children Avi, Leo, Esther, and Michael were, as usual, helpful in making our own family life a joyous one and encouraged us in this effort. The final copy was typed by Gwen Peroni.

CONTRIBUTORS

Beth Israel Hospital Elder Abuse Assessment Team, Boston, Mass.

Arthur Blank is the Director of Psychological Services, Queensway-Carleton Hospital in Ottawa, Ontario

Deborah Marks Conley is Gerontological Nurse Co-ordinator, University of Nebraska Medical Centre in Omaha, Nebraska

Paul Girard is the Director of Social Work, Victoria General Hospital in Halifax, Nova Scotia

Stanley E. Goldstein is chief in Psychiatry, Queensway-Carleton Hospital in Ottawa, Ontario

J. Edward Hudson is a doctoral student at the Faculty of Social Work, University of Toronto

Elizabeth Podnieks is on the Faculty of Nursing, Ryerson Polytechnical Institute in Toronto, Ontario

Gilbert Sharpe is on the Faculty of Health Sciences, McMaster University, Hamilton, Ontario

Rachel Schlesinger is in the Division of Social Sciences at York University, Toronto, Ontario

Benjamin Schlesinger is on the Faculty of Social Work, University of Toronto

Donna J. Shell is with the Manitoba Council on Aging, Winnipeg, Manitoba

Mish Vadasz is the senior consultant in Social Work at the
Vancouver Health Department, British Columbia

Abuse of the Elderly: Issues and Annotated Bibliography

The prosperity of a country can be seen simply in how it treats its old people.

Nachman of Bratslav

Do not dishonour the old: we shall all be numbered among them.

Ben Sirach, Ecclesiasticus 8:6

Just because I am old, do not forget me, do not neglect me.

Standard Prayer Book

'When I was a laddie/I lived with my granny/And many a hiding me granny gi'ed me/Now I am a man/And I live with my granny/And I do to my granny/What she did to me.'

Traditional Rhyme, anonymous.

1
GRANNYBASHING
RACHEL ABER SCHLESINGER

We are growing old. We read in the journals, newspapers and
reports from Statistics Canada that we are a greying population. In 1980, for example there were approximately 3.2
million Canadians aged 60 years or more (Statistics Canada,
1981). If projections are correct, moreover, this figure
will increase to 4.5 million by the turn of this century.
A striking additional fact is that the 1981 Census figures
revealed that there are far more women than men in this
group of the greying population. In 1986 there were 2.7
million Canadians over the age of 65.

Over half of Canada's women who are over the age of 70
years are widows. The world of the aging contains unique
factors. Senior citizens have greater health problems than
their younger counterparts, and they are part of a group
with an unusually large concentration of people with low
incomes. In short, we as women are living longer, sometimes
in poor health, and often in a state of poverty. An unusually
large number of our older sisters will be dependent on
family or on public supports. Social service programs, as
well as both public and private funding, cannot provide
sufficient housing for these elderly. More seniors will be
living with family members, and we will see an increase in
multi-generational households.

As women, we would dearly love to anticipate an ideal
future. We want to imagine living out our older years as
creative, alert, healthy individuals, living as we choose,
perhaps in family settings, perhaps in our own homes, in
co-operative apartment units, or perhaps we look forward to
living alone, on our own individual timetable. In actuality,
many of us will be living in institutions, in senior citizen
housing units, or with our children in joint households. The
facts indicate that as older parents live longer, they may

become dependent on their children, and this period of dependency upon their children will be of longer duration than the period during which their children were dependent upon them.

For a variety of factors such as poverty of individual and community resources, and health conditions, 'Granny' will be living with her children. What will these multi-generational households have in common? They will contain at least two working adults, since the trend towards more involvement in the workforce on the part of women is in-creasing. With both husband and wife working, there may be a shortage of care for the elderly, physically dependent person. Another factor of these households will be the pattern of aging. Modern medical care has helped us live longer. One result of this is that the caretaker is often herself over 65, and is caring for a mother who is in her eighties.

Growing old can include the joys of living a full life, of activity and participation of new beginnings and having a warm, supportive family and friends, a life of meeting new challenges. Or ... the life of the elderly can be bounded by borders of helplessness, fear, poverty and abuse. Our task in this paper is to bring to light a crime of abuse of the elderly in family settings.

The 1960s made us aware of the problems of child abuse. The 1970s focused attention on wife battering. In the 1980s we are becoming aware of still another form of family violence, one that the English have labelled 'Grannybashing' or 'Granslamming.' This problem must be acknowledged and named, for only then can it be confronted, and ways found to prevent this form of abuse.

> My husband died ten years ago. The house we lived in became mine ... My younger daughter who had two unfor-tunate marriages was welcomed by us with her children. That was eighteen years ago. The past three years things have gotten steadily worse. My daughter locked me in the garage and left me there ... Whenever I tried to cook a meal, she would appear and turn off the gas and remove the grills so that the only way I could cook was to hold the pan over the fire ... My daughter's treatment of me kept getting worse. Always hurting me physically and mentally, kicking me, pushing me, grappling with me ... She is a well educated person ... (Quoted in Eastman, 1984, p. 30).

5 Grannybashing

The abuse of the elderly in the private family setting is
difficult for outsiders to identify. The abused child is
often identified by a teacher or doctor. The beaten wife may
be seen by a neighbour, or she may seek help from a crisis
centre. It is not easy for the elderly, dependent, often
physically handicapped woman to seek relief from abuse. She
is often invisible. If she is not seen by neighbours and
friends, ill health can be given as a plausible reason for
her absence.

What constitutes abuse of the elderly?

It is difficult to pinpoint elderly abuse without providing
some basic definitions. Is this abuse physical in nature? Is
it psychological? Is it purposive or is it accidental? Does
neglect constitute abuse? Is abuse only that which is
repetitive, or can it also be limited to a single incident?
The definitions of abuse include all the above factors.
   Faulkner (1982) defines elderly abuse as relating to
abuse and neglect by primary caregivers within the home.
Others (Block and Sinnott, 1979) include three major categories of abuse: physical, psychological, and economic.
Physical abuse includes both bruises as well as lack of
supervision and proper care that can lead to injuries. Included in the category of psychological abuse are threats
and isolation. Stealing or cheating the elderly out of their
own·funds and possessions constitutes material or economic
abuse. Abuse can further be defined in terms of verbal and
emotional factors.
   Elderly abuse is similar to child abuse and wife
battering in many ways; the hurt can be physical, emotional
or verbal and it strikes individuals who are powerless to
prevent the hurt.
   Some abuse is considered criminal assault, while other
forms relate not to a specific action, but to neglect, the
failure to act and this failure to provide safe supervision
leads to abuse.

   Abuse is any act of commission or omission which results
   in harm to the elderly individual, and is not restricted
   to physical harm, but ... includes financial, psychological and social abuse (Shell, 1982, p. 1).

While abuse can take place within institutions that care
for the elderly, or assault can occur on the streets in the

form of a mugging or robbery, this paper will focus on the intra-familial abuse of the older adult. In our society, a small percentage of the elderly are being cared for in institutions. Elderly women are especially dependent on their families for daily care. They may never have worked, have few financial resources, and may be physically in-capable of living on their own as they get older.

Who are the victims?

Douglass (1983) identifies them as '... the older, elderly persons, frail, mentally or physically disabled, female and living with the person responsible for the abuse' (p. 367). In the United States it is estimated that one million elderly people may be victims of moderate to severe abuse (Shell 1982). We have few comparable Canadian statistics regarding abuse, but we do have the certainty that it is increasing.

Who abuses?

Reports from the United States House of Representatives Select Committee on Aging (Shell 1982) identifies the son of the victim as the most likely to abuse, followed by the daughter, and finally the spouse of the victim.

Why does family abuse of the elderly occur?

The answer to this question relates to family factors as well as to an understanding of the realities of the aging process. A 'typical' abuse scenario might run as follows:

> She is old and frail. She is poor, and is totally de-pendent on her children who live in her home. From time to time she gets confused and forgets things. One day she forgot what she was talking about, and even who she was talking to. She forgets to pay her bills. Her son is un-employed, and her daughter-in-law works the double shift of the overburdened housewife and worker. Her first shift is from 8:30 to 4:30 at the factory, and then she comes to the shift that lasts the rest of her waking hours. During her 'second shift' she cares for her family, including her mother-in-law. When there are money problems, overworked family members react with short tempers. When she forgets to eat, her son hits her

... and that is how it begins: grannybashing, or
gramslamming.

Written into this scenario are feelings of frustration
and conflict about the dependent mother. The physical
condition of this woman makes her victimization possible.
The victim is often blamed, in this case, for being old,
dependent, powerless, ill and frail. Economic factors also
trigger abuse. In a family where all the adults work there
is less supervision for the older person. Stress is added by
the higher medical and health costs incurred by 'Granny.'
This situation tends, moreover, to last for many years,
since we live longer and have a greater life expectancy.
Family difficulties can also arise due to the changed
status of the various family members. The mother may have
headed this family for many years, and now roles are re-
versed, she has lost her power and her particular functions
and roles within her family. Abusive families may contain
members who have a drug problem, a drinking problem, or
marital problems.
Another aspect that must be considered is the condition
of the aging process. Being frail and in ill health
heightens the sense of dependency, and creates a fear of
revealing abuse. In many cases the abused woman needs and
loves her family, and fears the loss of their support.
Some families abuse or neglect the older person owing to
a lack of understanding of how to care for this person. They
don't know how to cope with her frailties and ill health.
Other families are unable to handle the financial and emotional stress caused by having 'Granny' live with them in
an already overcrowded home, where money is scarce and privacy is at a premium.
One other major factor that relates to 'Grannybashing' is
the very startling realization that abuse is a learned response. There are learned patterns of violence and abuse,
caused by a family history of violence. The developmental
approach to abuse finds that adults who were abused as
children or wives, tend to be abusive themselves when
overwhelmed with stress or conflict situations (Shell,
1982). There is a 50 per cent chance that abused children
will themselves abuse their dependent parents (Star, 1980).

Mary Sumers who lives down your street, cannot walk alone
due to her crippling arthritis. She often stays in her
room all day, unable to eat because she can't manage to

get downstairs to the kitchen. No one brings her anything
before they all leave the house for the day. She is
unfed, and often unwashed. She is neglected, and afraid
to call attention to herself. She is afraid of being hit
again, her arm was broken last year by her daughter when
she called out in the middle of the night. She is afraid
of being sent away. She is a victim of her frailties,
her fears, and her humiliation due to her need to be
cared for.

Mary is similar to the women studied by Steuer and Austin
(1980). Abused persons, they found, were frail, between the
ages of 73-86 years, with physical and/or mental problems
that led to their dependence on others for food, medicine,
and hygiene. *Most were women.* Shell (1982) found that a
typically abused person is a woman, in her eighties, who has
been living with her family for a year or more. Her study
indicated that the most common form of abuse was financial,
followed by psychosocial abuse and then physical abuse. Included in the financial aspect were cashing pension cheques
and withholding the funds, and gaining control of the older
person's total financial resources. Verbal abuse fell in the
category of psychosocial as did isolation and confinement.
'It was not uncommon for elderly persons to be confined to
small, dark cold cellars, basements and bedrooms' (Shell,
1982, p. 43).
    Assault constituting physical abuse was often followed by
withholding food. 'Physical abuse ranged from severe
beatings, causing bruises, welts and fractures, to actual
homicides' (Shell, 1982, p. 43). This study, carried out by
the Manitoba Council on Aging, also concluded that a large
number of abusive caregivers were themselves over 60 years
of age (Shell, 1982). It seems clear that stress, overload,
and burnout occurs in relation to aging as well as in the
worlds of work.

What can be done?

The first step is to make the public aware of the varied
forms of 'private' or 'domestic' abuse of the
elderly. 'Granslamming' will remain hidden until the issues
can be dealt with. Families need help in dealing with the
stress they encounter in their lives *before* they abuse the
elderly in their midst. *Prevention* can be more useful than
intervention.

One form of prevention is *education*. Families can be
helped to understand the aging process better, and taught
ways to deal with the conditions of aging. Family members
can then better understand the limitations and the fears
faced by the elderly in their care. *Mutual support groups*
have emerged from the consciousness-raising groups of the
1970s. The ability to share problems and discuss possible
approaches built into a health and prevention model rather
than a 'problem or illness' model can be of great benefit.

Another step, further down the road, is to have mandatory
legislation that would provide legal protection for the
elderly. The final, and least favoured solution is to
provide referrals to the police and safe housing for the
abused elderly – a form of half-way house when all else
fails.

Douglass (1983) lists the solutions to elderly abuse
under three main headings: education, crisis intervention,
and advocacy.

It is clear that the family is experiencing change in
many areas, and needs help in caring for the older family
members. Families are not 'typical.' The 'Mary Sumers' of
today could be living with her married child, with a single-
parent family, or even in a blended family. The family that
is the primary caregiver for the aged, dependent woman is
varied in its forms and particular problems. Stress and
conflict exists, and the victim of abuse is often blamed
for contributing to her dependency. Specific help can be
given these families in routine matters. The family can get
support from meal preparation programs and from visiting
homemakers. Transportation help can be provided for the
older person to enable her to participate in day-care programs outside the home. Finally, tax incentives can be given
for those who care for an older adult within the home.

In Canada, we anticipate that by the turn of the century
one quarter of our population will be 'grey,' aged 60 years
and over. Will the Mary Sumers of the year 2000 be able to
look forward to peace, care, enjoyment and challenge after a
life of working both within the home and perhaps outside in
the workforce? Or will she face a slow death brought about
by abuse, neglect, fear and isolation? We must be aware of
the crime of elderly abuse, and we must begin to initiate
programs and attitudes to prevent it. We support rape crisis
centres, we fight to help the battered wife, and we speak
out against child abuse in all forms. We fight for a quality
of life. Why are we silent when our mothers and grandmothers

struggle alone and in silence in their battle for survival, for growing old in an atmosphere of dignity and understanding? We must provide the strength for those who no longer have much strength. We must hear the silent cries, and our voices must help them speak. We too will grow old, and we too want to live in a world of mutual respect, love and care, not increased elderly abuse, not a world of 'Grannybashing.'

References and a Selected Bibliography on Abuse of the Elderly

Block, M. and J. Sinnott, eds. *The Battered Elder Syndrome*. College Park, Maryland: University of Maryland Center on Aging, 1979.

Canadian Governmental Report on Aging. Government of Canada, June, 1982

Chaplin, Leslie. 'The Battered Elderly,' *Geriatrics*, July, 1982: 37(7)

Chen, P., S. Bell, D. Dolinsky, J. Doyle, and M. Dunn. 'Elderly Abuse in Domestic Settings: A Pilot Study,' *Journal of Gerontological Social Work*, Fall 1981:4(1)

Douglass, Richard, 'Domestic Neglect and Abuse of the Elderly: Implication for Research and Service,' *Family Relations*, 1983, 32: 395–402

Eastman, Peggy. 'Elders Under Siege,' *Psychology Today*, January, 1984, p. 30

Faulkner, Lawrence. 'Mandating the Reporting of Suspected Cases of Elder Abuse: An Inappropriate, Ineffective and Ageist Response to the Abuse of Older Adults,' *Family Law Quarterly*, Spring, 1982, 16: 69–92

Ferguson, Doris. 'Aged Abuse,' *Journal of Gerontolocial Nursing*, June, 1981, 7(6): 333–6

Finkelhor, D., R. Gelles, G. Hotaling, and M. Straus, eds. *The Dark Side of Families: Current Family Violence Research*. Sage Publications, Beverly Hills, 1983

Hindman, M.H. 'Family Violence: An Overview,' *Alcohol and Research World*, 1979, 4(1): 2–11

Hooyman, Nancy R. *Older Women as Victims of Family Violence*. University of Washington, 1980

Koch, Lewis and Joanne Koch. 'Parent Abuse – A New Plague,' *Parade*, 27, January, 1980.

Lau, E. and J. Kosberg. 'Abuse of the Elderly by Informal Careproviders,' *Aging*, 1979, 299: 10–15

'On Beating Grandmother,' *New York Times*, 16 November, 1976,
   41
Pedrick-Cornell, C. and R. Gelles. 'Elder Abuse: The Status
   of Current Knowledge,' *Family Relations*, 1982, 31: 457-65
Rathbone-McCuan, Eloise. 'Elderly Victims of Family Violence
   and Neglect,' *Social Casework*, 1980, 61: 296-304
Shell, Donna. *Protection of the Elderly: A Study of Elder
   Abuse*. Manitoba Council on Aging, 1982.
Select Committee on Aging. U.S. House of Representatives,
   U.S. Government Printing Office, 1980.
Star, B. 'Patterns in Family Violence,' *Social Casework*,
   1980, 61: 339-46
Steinmetz, S. 'Elder Abuse,' *Aging*, Jan.-Feb. 1981, 6-10
------. 'Battered Parents,' *Society*, 15:5, July-Aug. 1978,
   54-5
Steuer, J. and E. Austin. 'Family Abuse of the Elderly,'
   Journal of the American Geriatrics Society, 28:8, 1980,
   372-6
The Elderly in Ontario: An Agenda for the 1980s. Toronto:
   Ontario Government Secretariat for Social Development,
   1981.
Walshe-Brennan, K. 'Granny Bashing,' *Nursing Mirror*, 22
   Dec. 1977.

2
ELDER ABUSE: AN OVERVIEW
J. EDWARD HUDSON

Within the memory of most of us, the elders - grandparents,
great aunts and uncles - were among the most revered relatives and members of society. The elderly could, in most
cases, look forward to an old age surrounded by the love and
care of their children and grandchildren. Hopefully, even
today, that holds true for the majority, whether the elderly
are able to remain in their own homes, live with family, or,
by choice or necessity, enter an institution. However, there
is a growing body of evidence in professional and popular
literature that from 2 to 4 per cent of our elderly will be
subjected to violence by a family member, a 'friend,' or a
neighbour.
    Elder abuse is not a new phenomenon. Most likely it existed
in the past, but there was, and still is, some reluctance to
concede its existence and its causes. It *is* happening, and
society, the professions, families, and concerned citizens
are only beginning to realize - or admit - it. The question
of elder abuse in institutions by trusted caretakers has of
late been shouted 'on the rooftops' by journalists reminis-
cent of the Old Testament prophets daring to say the un-
thinkableé This paper has no prophetic overtones, but will
consider the notion of elder abuse, will look at familial
and institutional abuse in greater depth, and finally will
note some implications for social work practice.

The notion of elder abuse

The notion of elder abuse comprises its definition and its
categories.

Definition
Although definitions of elder abuse are multiple and vary
from author to author (Giordano & Giordano, 1984; Pedrick-

Cornell & Gelles, 1982), Kimsey et al. (1981), quoting Levine (1978), have come up with one of the most comprehensive:

> abuse ... is any action on the part of an elderly
> person's family (family being defined as any relatives
> related by blood, marriage or adoption, and any
> associated persons who have daily household contact, such
> as a housekeeper or roommate, or any person upon whom the
> elder is reliant for his daily needs of food, clothing,
> or shelter), or a professional caretaker to take
> advantage of his person, property, or emotional being
> through threat of violence, use of violence, or use of
> disciplinary restraints (i.e., physical and chemical
> strait-jacketing), or negligence on the part of the
> caretaker to provide basic needs. We designate a person
> as elderly, if age 60 or older (466).

This definition includes both violence to and *neglect* of the elderly and their categories *according to source* (*informal caretakers*, i.e., family or those assimilated to family; *formal caretakers* or professionals) and *type* (physical, psychological, material, etc.). The categories of elder abuse according to source will be dealt with in the second part of this paper and attention is now directed to the categories according to type, irrespective of the setting of the abuse.

Categories according to type
Just as there is little agreement about a definition of elder abuse, so, too, writers diverge in discussing its types. Falcioni (1982) mentions physical, psychological, material abuse, and violation of rights; Giordano and Giordano (1984) and Schlesinger (1985) enumerate physical and psychological abuse, negligence, financial exploitation, violation of rights, and self-neglect; Pedrick-Cornell and Gelles (1982) refer to passive and active neglect, mental anguish, medical abuse, and self-abuse; and Schell (1982) speaks of financial, psychological, and physical abuse. It appears that all the above are, at times, naming or dividing the categories differently but addressing the same realities. Kimsey et al. (1981) have categorized the types of abuse under *four* main headings (468-471): physical, psychological, material, and fiscal, each of which will be explained briefly.
    Physical abuse. The most obvious and usually demonstrable category, physical abuse may result in an elderly person's

being burned, bruised, hit/punched, raped (homosexually or
heterosexually), scratched, slapped, and whipped. Injuries
may range from unexplained contusions to broken bones and
internal injuries. Besides intentional assault, physical
neglect as a subtype of physical abuse seems far more common
than deliberate injury, and its effects may be even more
far-reaching where neglect involves failure to administer
proper medication or to provide an appropriate diet.

   Psychologic abuse. It is easier to describe psychologic
abuse than to define it, as it comprises several subcatego-
ries, some of which overlap with more physical manifestations
of abuse. For example, the *condition of the facility* in terms
of interior maintenance and/or cleanliness should be of such
standard as to reduce the effects of environmental deprivation
on the affective, cognitive, and intellectual functioning of
the elderly. *Inadequate diet* may be viewed as another form
of environmental deprivation and psychologic abuse. *Grooming*
is important even to the elderly and its *neglect* tends to
reinforce a negative self-image. Furthermore, it is demeaning
and demoralizing to see one's peers in states of disarray and
poor hygiene. Impersonal and mechanistic care constitutes
'abuse by benign neglect' and is a further assault on the
dignity of an elderly person. *Verbal abuse* (threats, insults,
mortification of the ego) can cause invisible, but none the
less, real wounds which never heal. *Infantilization* may
result from regression brought on by a combination of
'transplantation shock' (due to an elderly person's being
uprooted and moved elsewhere involuntarily), verbal abuse,
environmental deprivation, and benign neglect.

   Material abuse. Thefts of the material possessions of the
elderly are widespread both in and out of institutions.
Theft of personal items and of patients' drugs are frequent
complaints.

   Fiscal abuse. Elderly patients who are dependent and
perhaps not too clear-minded may be subjected to fraud and
embezzlement not only by family members but by formal caregivers as well. The following are examples: embezzlement
of trust funds; improper charges for services or for services never performed; billing for drugs never supplied,
billing for trade-name drugs but dispensing generic substi-
tutions, billing for the prescribed strength of a drug but
dispensing a lesser strength; and failure to notify the
Province or State that a patient has left or died, so that
billing may continue for the patient's room, etc.

Elder abuse according to source

The purpose here is to explore more in detail elder abuse as
it originates with family members and close familial associates (informal caregivers) and, secondly, as it originates
with professionals (formal caregivers) in the different
settings in which they work.

Abuse by informal caregivers
Elder abuse by informal caregivers is also termed *family-
mediated* or *domestic*. It is within this area that various
(popular) terms have been coined by journalists and professionals in an attempt both to shock the public and raise
their awareness: battered elder syndrome, battered parent
syndrome, family violence unto elders, grandparent abuse,
'granny-bashing', 'gramslamming', etc. (Rathbone-McCuan &
Voyles, 1982; Schlesinger, 1984). It is a sad paradox that,
in the 1980s, when life expectancy is greater than it ever
has been (by the year 2000, it is projected those 65 and
over will make up 11 per cent of the Canadian population
[Rose, 1981]), the elderly living with their families are
exposed to the threat of and actually experience abuse. Incidents of domestic abuse have also been reported by nursing
home personnel: 'One local medical society [received] three
calls from nursing homes in a single week, wanting to know
[how] they could prevent family members from physically
abusing the parent during visiting hours' (Steinmetz, 1978,
54).
   O'Malley et al. (1983), in commenting on the definition
of family-mediated abuse, have underlined 'the characteristic
common to all described cases, namely the abnormal expression
of the caretaking role in which the needs of a person for
physical and emotional support are increased or ignored'
(1000). On this basis, he has operationalized the following:
'*Neglect*: Failure of a caretaker to intervene to resolve
significant need despite awareness of available resources.
Abuse: *Active* intervention by a caretaker such that unmet
needs are created or sustained with resultant physical,
psychological, or financial injury' (1000, emphasis added).
As seen earlier, such needs include physical requirements
for shelter, food, clothing and medical care: needs for
assistance in feeding, bathing, toileting, dressing, ambu-
lating, communicating, cleaning, shopping, managing medica-
tions and finances; and emotional needs such as stimulation,
support, and protection from threat or harm.

Incidence. The extent of elder abuse in Canada is not known, but the research done by Schell (1982) in Manitoba support studies in the United States where it is estimated from half a million to 2.5 million elderly people each year may be the victims of different kinds of moderate to severe domestic abuse (Health & Welfare Canada, 1983: Vadasz, 1985). This abuse is being carried out by relatives, neighbours, and friends. Evidence suggests it is difficult to detect and document physical abuse (for which the 500,000 annual figure is given for the U.S.) (Kimsey et al., 1981), let alone psychological abuse. The elderly victims of family violence may be living in relative isolation or fear of being abandoned or placed in an institution. Too, there is always the dread of reprisals or the stigma of reporting a son or a daughter. Furthermore, some severe mental or physical impairment may prevent them from reporting the abuse. Not the least important, professionals may be slow to admit the phenomenon exists [particularly in smaller centres] (Health & Welfare Canada; Rathbone-McCuan, 1980).

Types. Some descriptive studies (e.g., Beck & Ferguson, 1981; Rathbone-McCuan & Voyles, 1982; Steinmetz, 1978) report the elderly's having suffered the range of abuse from physical to fiscal without giving percentages for different types. On the other hand, Schell (1982) stated 'The type of abuse most frequently encountered was financial, followed by psychosocial [psychologic] and physical' (43). Recognizing overlap between these three categories, she also did not mention percentages. Hickey and Douglass (1981), after interviewing 228 professionals about their care experience with abuse and neglect of the elderly, found that 'only 77 (38.7 per cent) of the 228 respondents reported *no* regular experience with physical abuse, and virtually no one was unfamiliar with one of the other categories of neglect and abuse' (173). Lau and Kosberg (1979b) found that 10 per cent of 404 elderly clients at a chronic illness centre were victims of physical abuse or neglect by a family member. In a study of only 12 abused persons (9 of whom were women), Steuer and Austin (1980) found primarily physical and verbal abuse, with neglect (e.g., leaving the victim unattended for long periods) being the most common form of abuse.

Profile. What are the characteristics of the abused and the abuser? Based on her study of 400 cases of reported elder abuse in Manitoba, Schell (1982) found that about two-thirds of the abused elderly were women averaging 80-84 years of age who lived with a family member for 10 years or

more. Three-quarters of the abusers were family members, 60
per cent being males. The son was the most frequent abuser
followed closely by the daughter. About one-third of the
abusers were in the over-60 age range, exemplifying perhaps
the many frustrations of aging caregivers. O'Malley et al.
(1983), reporting on their review of several descriptive and
empirical studies on family-mediated elder abuse, found
agreement as follows: victims are predominantly female;
those over age 75 years have disproportionately more reported abuse than others and women outnumber men in all age
groups. Seventy-five per cent have significant physical or
mental impairment and are unable to meet their daily needs
without assistance. In 60 per cent of case reports, the
elderly person is a significant source of stress to the
abuser. In 75 per cent of reported cases, the abuser has
other significant stresses such as alcoholism, chronic
medical problems, or financial crises. The abuser is a
relative in 86 per cent of the reports and lives with the
elderly person in 75 per cent. Bookin and Dunkle (1985),
from their literature review and practice experience,
confirm the findings of O'Malley et al. Rathbone-McCuan
(1980), based on a review of domestic elder abuse in her own
practice, has come up with a similar summary profile of
abused and abuser, i.e.:

> [...] the following list of characteristics appear to be
> relevant in the majority of cases: 1. The victim is
> female. 2. The victim is sixty-five years or older.
> 3. The victim is functionally dependent because of
> inadequate resources or physical limitations. 4. There
> is a history of alcoholism, retardation, or psychiatric
> illness for either the caregiver or the elderly person.
> 5. There is a history of inter- and intra-generational
> conflict. 6. There is a previous history of related
> incidents (300).

No generalizable empirical studies specifically on the
relation of ethnic factors to family-mediated elder abuse
could be found. However, Bookin and Dunkle (1985) have
pointed out that cultural influences of all those involved
in the identification process (the professional, the abused
elder, his or her family, significant others) come into play
when the investigation of possible maltreatment starts.
Values and attitudes 'are shaped by the norms, values, and
cultural influences operant in society at large and in his

or her own family system' (6). At the same time, they quote
a study by Ann Langley (1981) on abuse of the elderly:
'Elder abuse is believed to cross all social, ethnic, socio-
economic, and education strata' (6). Hence, given the heter-
ogeneity of the population, profiles of abused and abuser
have limited utility.

Theories on domestic elder abuse
There are many theories or explanations for domestic elder
abuse (Lau & Kosberg, 1979a), none of which is completely
satisfactory because of the lack of empirical evidence
(Pedrick-Cornell & Gelles, 1982). Vieno (1983) has hypothesized that 'The victimization of the elderly must, indeed,
be placed within the context in which aging itself has been
made into a process of progressive victimization. [...] in
[North] America society, for example, becoming old means
becoming less of something on the way to losing everything'
(13). In fact, much of the theoretical framework on elder
abuse comprises propositions and theories borrowed from
other forms of intrafamilial abuse (Block & Sinnott, 1979,
in Giordano & Giordano, 1984). Giordano and Giordano (234-5)
have given one of the best and most recent summaries of
seven different hypotheses bearing on familial elder abuse
(a number of these factors have been emphasized under 'profile' of abused and abuser):

Family dynamics. Violence is a normative behavioural
pattern learned in the context of the family. *One in 400*
children reared nonviolently attacks their parents later on,
compared to *1* out of *2* children mistreated violently by
their parents (Rathbone-McCuan, 1980; Steinmetz, 1978).

Impairment and dependence. Elderly women with severe
physical or mental impairments are the most likely to be
abused (Burston, 1975). Impairments lead to dependence
making the person vulnerable to abuse (O'Rourke, 1981),
although some think the normal dependency of the elderly is
sufficient to make them vulnerable to such abuse (Douglass,
Hickey, & Noel, 1980).

Personality traits of the abuser. The third hypothesis
holds that the abuser is inclined to be abusive due to
personality traits or a characterial disorder. Research has
neither conclusively confirmed nor refuted this, but it
seems clear personality traits of the abusing person are
still a factor to be considered (O'Rourke, 1981).

Filial crisis. Elder abuse may result from the failure of
adult children to resolve the filial crisis, in that they

have not gone beyond the stage of adolescent rebellion
toward emancipation from their parents. Hence, parent-child
conflicts originating in adolescence continue into later
life (Block & Sinnott, 1979; Farrar, 1955; Lau & Kosberg,
1979a).

Internal stress. The responsibility of caring for a
dependent, elderly relative can provoke family stress which
can in turn result in abuse (Block & Sinnott, 1979; Rathbone-
McCuan, 1980). When caregivers spend many hours per week
providing physical and psychological assistance to a frail
elderly relative, not surprisingly do they become anxious
and exhausted. They may also become resentful, angry, and
frustrated or feel they are prevented from seeing to the
needs of other members of the family.

External stress. In the 1970s, research on family violence recognized external stress on the family as a major
contributing factor to violence. Several correlates of
violence were identified: age, income level, employment
status, urban-rural residence. Abusers of relatives were
likely to be alcoholics experiencing some form of external
stress, such as loss of job or a longterm medical problem.
External stressors, such as life crises and environmental
factors, also trigger abuse (Douglass, Hickey, & Noel, 1980;
Legal Research and Services for the Elderly, 1979).

Negative attitudes toward the elderly. Patterns of
familial elder abuse are apt to be reinforced by negative
stereotyping of the elderly and their societal roles. Expectations can distort perceptions. The resulting misperceptions
can be a major force in creating situations conducive to
abuse. Negative attitudes pave the way to dehumanization of
the elderly and facilitate victimization with the abusers
feeling remorse (Block & Sinnott, 1979; Kalish, 1979; Vieno,
1983).

Abuse by formal caregivers
In November 1985, the Toronto Star newspaper, in a five-part
series, examined issues affecting the day-to-day living of
the 29,000 elderly and frail residents in Ontario's private
nursing homes. Instances of serious abuse and neglect were
cited (Harvey, 4 November 1985). Only since the beginning
1980s have journal articles more seriously broached the
subject of elder abuse and neglect by professionals or
formal caregivers, also termed 'institutional abuse,
neglect, and mistreatment' (Doty & Sullivan, 1983, 223;
Goldstein & Blank, 1982; Halamandaris, 1983; Kimsey et al.,

1981; Podnieks, 1983; Solomon, 1983; Tarbox, 1983). Doty and
Sullivan found, for example, that 'it is not uncommon for
problems of patient abuse, neglect, and mistreatment in
nursing homes to be dismissed on the grounds the evidence
is anecdotal. The implication is that a journalist or a
politician "on the make" can always go out and uncover a
"horror story" or two' (223). It is important, then, to be
able to document a pattern of abuse, which they have described as a 'wide range of problems - everything from
garden variety lack of courtesy and helpfulness to outright
physical abuse' (223), by formal caregivers, i.e., those
'professionally trained in delivering health care, who work
in an institutional setting. Such caretakers include but are
not limited to physicians, nurses, social workers, and
administrators. The settings are chiefly hospitals and
nursing homes' (Kimsey et al., 466).

   Incidence. Neither the Manitoba study by Schell (1982)
nor Health and Welfare Canada (1983) have dealt with
institutional elder abuse and neglect. Goldstein and Blank
(1982), without mentioning statistics, have alluded to abuse
allegedly taking place in Canadian institutions, but, in an
attempt to exonerate these last, stated: 'institutions for
the elderly have a difficult task and are often used as
scapegoats by relatives and patients. [...] Thus, these
caregivers are abused and unable to counterattack' (456).
Similarly, Harvey (4 November 1985) has reported: '[...]
according to the nursing homes' association [Ontario], the
picture of nursing homes as substandard, uncaring institutions is false' (A1). Yet the journalist west on to say:

> Visits by the Star to 14 [randomly chosen] Metro-area
> nursing homes found evidence to support complaints made
> to a task force on health care, funded by the Canadian
> Medical Association. The cross-country task force, headed
> by consumer reporter Joan Watson, concluded that many of
> Canada's nursing homes had serious problems: 'The stand-
> ard of care in many ... is grossly inadequate.' Last
> month [October 1985], the Christian Labour Association
> of Canada released a task force report on conditions in
> Ontario nursing homes [...]. Based on interviews with
> staff, owners, and administrators, the task force con-
> cluded that many nursing homes are badly underfunded
> and understaffed; and conditions in some are inhumane.
> [...] [Furthermore], since 1980, Ontario coroners have
> ordered 23 inquests into nursing-home-related deaths

[details given of malnutrition, dehydration, and
neglect]. [...] In the 84-85 fiscal year, [...] 582
charges were laid against 17 nursing homes (A19).

Goldstein and Blank's defence of Canadian institutions
notwithstanding, there *is evidence* of institutional elder
abuse in Canada. Podnieks (1983) confirms this: 'When I
first started to research certain well documented examples
of elder abuse, neglect, and exploitation [by nursing
staff], I was deeply shocked' (34).

In the United States, a number of general and statistical
studies on the incidence of elderly abuse have appeared.
Doty and Sullivan (1983) have quoted figures attesting that,
as of September 29, 1980, '7 per cent of SNFs [skilled
nursing facilities/nursing homes] nationwide (N=550 facilities with 53,936 beds) has been cited [by a federal certi-
fication agency] as deficient on the requirement that
patients' rights, policies and procedures ensure that each
patient admitted to the facility is free from mental and
physical abuse and free from chemical and (except in emer-
gencies) physical restraints except as authorized in writing
by a physician [...]' (224). The researchers also found that
'7 per cent of SNFs nationwide (N=539 facilities with 57,228
beds) were cited as deficient on the requirement that each
patient "is treated with consideration, respect, and full
[...] dignity"' (224). Statistics documenting institutional
abuse or neglect in individual states are also cited.
Halamandaris (1983) has mentioned 'documented widespread
fraud and abuse among nursing homes participating in the
Medicaid program. [...] In 1980, [...] 3,067 cases of potential Medicaid fraud [were] being investigated by the
states' (104-5). Kimsey et al. have lamented that 'Numerous
studies point to antipathy toward the aged on the part of
professionals' (465), later translating into abuse of the
aged: 'Reports in the mass media are increasing, particularly
[regarding] abuses in the nursing home population'(466).

Types. Harvey (4-6 November 1985) either personally
observed or was told of a wide range of elder abuse in the
14 Metro-Toronto area nursing homes visited. This included
physical abuse of residents by staff or other residents,
this type of abuse along with *material abuse* (theft of
personal belongings) being least common. There were multiple
instances of what could be termed *psychologic abuse*, including poor nursing care or neglect: verbal abuse of residents by staff; threats; lack of privacy and respect for

the dignity of residents; poor diet; lack of attention to
residents' grooming or personal hygiene; lack of supervision; falsification of patients' charts, called 'lie-sheets'
by some staff; unnecessary enemas; unnecessary physical restraints; doctors' orders ignored, etc.

Returning again to the research on institutional elder
abuse in the United States, Doty (1983) gives examples from
New York City nursing homes: a patient suffered serious leg
burns; a resident was overmedicated; several residents
unable to feed themselves were not being fed; unsanitary
conditions were noted, etc. Halamandaris (1983) specifies
several types of fiscal abuse (fraud) being perpetrated in
nursing homes across the U.S.: theft of patients' funds,
collecting for dead or discharged patients, fraudulent
therapy charges, fraudulent pharmaceutical charges, kick-
backs, etc. Kimsey et al. (1981) and Tarbox (1983) present
data from a comprehensive study on the 1,000 nursing homes
in Texas: 'Deliberate physical abuse by formal caretakers
was least common; physical neglect was far more common,
e.g., development of [bedsores], inadequate nutrition, improper medication, and vermin infestation. Psychologic abuse
was most frequent in the area of benign neglect, with
patients regarded as "going to die anyway"' (Kimsey et al.,
465). There was also theft of personal belongings along with
embezzlement of patients' trust funds.

Profile. Podnieks (1983) has spoken of the 'vulnerability
[of the abused patient] apparent in his physical frailty,
his dangerously low self esteem and lack of self confidence.
He is an easy target for the frustration, hostility, and
scorn of [his caregivers] [...]' (34). Kimsey et al. (1981)
have delineated the characteristics of the total nursing
home population in Texas (N=76,834): average age is 82, with
95 per cent over 65 and 70 per cent over 79; women outnumber
men, two to one; most patients are poor and isolated; half
have no close relatives; more than 50 per cent have some
mental impairment; and fewer than 50 per cent can walk
alone. This gives some idea of the profile of persons who
may be subjected to institutional abuse. They share many of
the characteristics of those abused by their own families.
There is little information on the profile of the abuser,
i.e., the formal caretaker. It has been hypothesized that
the abuser in institutions may resemble his/her counterpart
in the domestic scene, i.e., may be dealing with unresolved
conflicts in his/her own family, frustration, etc. Some
observers see the abuser as a poorly paid aide or orderly

working long hours and in poor working conditions. Discour-
agement, depression, and denial are also operative (Kimsey
et al.). No detailed portrait of the abusing/neglectful
nurse, physician, social worker, therapist, or administrator
exists.

Theories. Although no satisfyingly comprehensive theory
has appeared to explain institutional elder abuse, some of
the hypotheses invoked to elucidate family mediated abuse
seem equally applicable here: *impairment and dependence*
(Burston, 1975; Douglass, Hickey, & Noel, 1980); *personality
traits of the abuser* (O'Rourke, 1981); *internal stress*
(Block & Sinnott, 1979); *external stress* (Legal Research and
Services for the Elderly, 1979); and *negative attitudes*
toward the elderly on the part of society and professionals
(Kalish, 1979; Vieno, 1983). Solomon's work (1983) on the
economic, role (stereotyping), attitudinal, and physical
victimization of the elderly by health professionals has
contributed to the understanding of the 'why' of institutional
abuse. Political attitudes, resulting in underfunding, under-
staffing, and inadequate nursing home or hospital facilities
are also an important, but often overlooked, consideration
(Kimsey et al., 1981).

Implications for social work practice

Are social workers aware of the extent of domestic and
institutional elder abuse? This is difficult to assess,
since the literature in the last eight years has originated
with, in the main, other professionals: physicians, nurses,
psychologists, lawyers, and sociologists. A search of *Social
Work Research and Abstracts* and other sources covering
1977-1985 turned up eight journal articles by social workers
concerning some aspect of elder abuse: Bookin and Dunkle,
1985; Giordano and Giordano, 1984; Hooyman, 1982; Pratt et
al., 1983; Rathbone-McCuan, 1980; Rathbone-McCuan and
Voyles, 1982; Schlesinger, 1985; and Tomita, 1982. Among
concerns raised were: 'the lack of a universally accepted
definition' of elder abuse (Bookin & Dunkle, p.3); the lack
of 'legal tools and support of community based services to
meet the needs [of the abused elderly]' (Bookin & Dunkle,
p.3; Pratt et al.); and the 'minimal research related to the
nature, extent and causes of elderly abuse [...] especially
[in Canada]' (Schlesinger, p. 15). Pedrick-Cornell and
Gelles (1982) have likewise complained about the 'very
little in the way of scholarly knowledge on this topic, [so

that] practitioners cannot presently locate quality research
knowledge [...] informative for their clinical practice'
(464). They, too, point out the dearth of 'established
resources, services, and treatment programs which can be
adopted, copied, or applied to the problem' (464). Acknowledging the above deficiencies, it is still both possible and
necessary to draw up some guidelines on the role of social
work in the assessment of and intervention in elder abuse
cases.

Assessment
Bookin and Dunkle (1985) highlight the *problem of identifying*
family-mediated elder abuse, not only due to lack of a clear
definition of same, but because of 'the worker's lack of
awareness or knowledge about elder abuse, [as] also his or
her personal and cultural biases'(4), an issue raised
earlier in this paper. Agencies and individuals, furthermore, may lack 'clear-cut guidelines regarding what degree
of maltreatment constitutes abuse' (4). For example, a
survey of physicians at a Seattle medical centre found that
the group sampled 'failed to agree unanimously on even one
element to be included in the definition of elder abuse'
(4). Supposing a case of suspected abuse has been identified, even then the worker may have only limited access to
the abused person, often living with the abuser. The abused
person, viewed by law as a consenting adult in the absence
of contrary evidence, may refuse examination by a physician
or nurse or any further help from the worker for fear of
retaliation by the abuser, who can easily threaten institutionalization (Bookin & Dunkle).

Rathbone and Voyles (1982) give some 'Case Detection
Guidelines' (190-2) where an elderly person is being abused
by informal caregivers. Their approach is based on the
practitioner's having access to the home and the opportunity
to observe 'the behavior of the aged person and the suspected abuser' (190). They emphasize the importance of
understanding *physical indicators* as the first and perhaps
key aspect of case detection. These indicators are 'observ-
able conditions of the aged person [e.g. bedsores, signs of
malnourishment, bruises, burns, lacerations, head injuries,
etc.] that range from signs of physical neglect to obvious
physical injury' (190). Cases of abuse may also be detected
from *behavioural observation*. How do the abuser and abused
person interact? Is the elderly person unduly afraid of the
adult child? 'Generalized and unusually high-level fear is

common in [abuse] situations' (191). The suspected abuser
may attempt to hide abuse by being oversolicitous while the
worker is present or again may exhibit aggressive, destructive, threatening behaviour in the worker's presence and
even towards the worker. 'A clinician must learn to recognize when the interview should end' (191) and decide whether
assessment can continue at some future time or whether
action should be initiated at once to protect the abused
person. In this latter case, clear documentation is needed,
and, if time and the situation permits, consultation with
one's agency and even legal counsel should be sought. Anything less may leave the worker open to charges of harass-
ment of abused and/or abuser, preclude further access to the
abused person, and open the possibility of yet more serious
harm to the one abused.

Falcioni (1982) has given attention to a multiprofes-
sional approach to assessment while emphasizing the role of
the nurse. Her detailed scheme would be more appropriate for
assessing abuse of someone admitted to hospital after
domestic abuse, although she does not state this. O'Malley
et al. (1983) likewise believe in a multidisciplinary approach involving the medical, social service, mental health,
and legal professions. They too, highlight the difficulties
inherent in identifying elder abuse and gaining access to
the abused person still at home. The problem of first access
is resolved when abuse is identified during the course of
visit to a doctor's office, emergency department, social
service agency, or on admission to hospital.

Tomita (1982) describes a protocol for 'Identification
and Assessment of Elder Abuse and Neglect' (45-50). The
protocol was developed by an interdisciplinary team composed
of a nurse, a mental health counsellor, a social worker, and
a physician at Harborview Medical Center, University of
Washington, Seattle. It was meant to '(1) improve the health
care professionals' detection, assessment and documentation
of both abusive and high-risk families; and (2) to assist
the professional in developing appropriate interventions for
victims of abuse' (39). It is designed for use with all
disciplines with each contributing a piece of information to
the composite assessment. Schell (1982) has reproduced a
somewhat similar but shorter protocol in use at Seven Oaks
General Hospital, Winnipeg, to identify circumstances which
may indicate abuse or neglect and to alert staff and discharge planners 'to the need for measures or resources which
can alleviate or reduce risk factors in the patients' living

arrangement' (58). Both the above protocols are geared to
in- or out-patient hospital assessment, although they could,
with adaptation, be used in home settings as well. The
literature surveyed lacks detailed protocols for assessment
of abuse in home settings.

How is institutional elder abuse assessed? Why is the
literature depressingly silent on this point with one small
exception? Champlin (1982), not a health professional but an
associate editor and a writer on geriatric issues, makes one
oblique reference to a protocol developed by emergency room
nurses at Beth Israel Hospital, Boston, to identify possible
physical abuse. '[...] most of the abuse victims they see at
the hospital are elderly persons suffering neglect in long-
term-care settings' (116). In addition to looking for physical clues of abuse or neglect, they also look for 'medica-
tions that are inappropriate to the patient's condition. The
most obvious is restraint-by-medication' (116). Who is going
to identify and assess elderly abuse taking place in hospitals or nursing homes? Are the staff going to police themselves? Certainly they need to, but such a course is fraught
with difficulties given the vested interest they may have in
maintaining the status quo, not to mention their own jobs.
Visiting staff in any profession should be aware of the
possibility of institutional abuse and be willing to take
steps to correct it. Social workers with their reputation
for advocacy can play a key role in such detection by
raising their own and other staff's consciousness to the
possibility of such abuse, and by encouraging a team
approach to its assessment.

Intervention
As with assessment, the bulk of the literature speaks to
interventive strategies in case of domestic elder abuse.
Both the social work publications and the literature of
other professions (medicine, nursing, psychology, law) deal
with intervention on the micro, mezzo, and/or macro levels.
There is general agreement that, if the victim's health
(physical, mental) and/or life are being seriously endan-
gered, then he/she should be removed from the setting or at
least from contact with the abuser. The need for legal advice to protect the rights of all concerned is also acknowledged. There is, besides, emphasis on the requirement to
consider the abuser, to reduce stress in the familial environment, and to introduce supports from the community
(help from neighbours, meals-on-wheels, homemakers, visiting

nurses, etc.). Too often, too little attention has been paid
to alleviating the cause(s) of the abuse as it relates to
the caretaker (Bookin & Dunkle, 1985; Giordano & Giordano,
1984; Hooyman, 1982; Lau & Kosberg, 1979; Pratt et al.,
1983; Schlesinger, 1985). O'Malley et al. have come up with
two models of intervention (see Appendix III & IV), one for
cases of family-mediated abuse 'in which the elderly person
has physical or mental impairments and is dependent on the
family for daily care needs' (1003), and the other for cases
'in which care needs are minimal or overshadowed by the
pathological behavior of the "non-normal caregiver"' (1003-4).

Intervention at the *mezzo* and *macro* levels is visualized
in terms of networking; educating professionals, politicians,
families of the elderly, local communities, and society at
large to the possibility, frequency, and deleterious effects
(at all levels) of elder abuse; and lobbying for legislation
not only for protective services for the elderly, – but for
expanded community social services: to meet the needs of the
growing elderly population and their caregivers, to follow
up cases of abuse, and to put in place effective preventive
measures (education, counselling services, support networks,
etc.) (Bragg et al., 1981; Champlin, 1982; Douglass, 1983;
Edwards, 1985; Tomita, 1982). Lawrence Faulkner (1982),
attorney and executive-director, Legal Services for the
Elderly Project of Erie County and Western New York, Inc.,
has very lucidly spelled out (and is one of the few to do
so) the inappropriateness and ineffectiveness of mandating
by law the reporting of suspected cases of elder abuse
without making the needed supportive services (financial,
health, nutrition, psychological, housing, etc.) available
to the aged and their caretakers.

Only a few writers, none of whom are social workers, have
spoken at some length of intervention in institutional abuse
cases. However, the majority of interventive strategies
recommended above for family-mediated abuse (removal of
abused person, counselling and support for abuser to alleviate stress, education at all levels, legislation) are also
applicable here. Bragg et al. (1981) pointed out the need
for *the legal community* as a whole (legislators, administrators, and lawyers) to confront the problem by making elder
abuse and neglect unlawful, by providing for the recovery of
damages from nursing homes and such, and by stipulating
either a fine for abuse or neglect, or a reward incentive
for superior nursing care. Doty (1983) sees *more active
community involvement* (friends and relatives associations,

ombudsman programs, community receiverships, mandatory abuse reporting, private and class action lawsuits) as a possible remedy against institutional abuse or neglect. Tarbox, based on his research that psychological abuse and neglect are the most prevalent form in nursing homes, stresses ways to reduce this: enriching the environment (by adding a few amenities) and minimizing infantilization, educating the community and increasing their involvement, an interdisciplinary approach to 'restorative care', and educating professionals and looking to improving their morale. In the province of Ontario, health minister Murray Elston said changes were on the horizon. 'One reform being considered is a *legislated residents' bill of rights*. This would guarantee, among other things, the right to privacy, the right to refuse treatment, and [above all] the right to *courteous treatment*. Elston says the province is [also] considering an independent advocacy system for nursing homes' (Harvey, 6 November 1985, p. A23, emphasis added).

Summary and conclusion

Over the last five years, the helping professions including social work have gradually recognized that abuse and neglect of the elderly constitute the third hideous segment of the family violence composite, in some senses more repulsive and shocking than child or spouse battering. The legal, medical, and nursing professions have out-stripped social work in the breadth and depth of their studies on family-mediated elder abuse. However, there are signs that, within the last two years at least, social work theorists and practitioners are seriously addressing domestic elder abuse in terms of its causes, detection, and prevention. This is a hopeful sign, but there is yet a great need to educate future social workers and those already practising in a model specific to social work and adapted to the needs of the elderly and their families.

None of the professions, except in a very few isolated instances, have adequately treated institutional maltreatment and neglect of older persons. Only the journalists have dared to bring the issue out into the open. Now that it has been exposed in all its ugliness, perhaps professionals, politicians, and the public will work towards a solution, which is personal, political, and social. Rathbone-McCuan and Voyles (1982) have best summarized the pathos in all forms of elder abuse: 'Violence is America's sweetheart, but

the elderly are not, and they pay a heavy price as victims
of societal neglect and blatant discrimination' (192).

References

Beck, C.M. and D. Ferguson. 'Aged Abuse,' *Journal of
  Gerontological Nursing*, 1981, 7: 333-6
Block, M.R. and J.D. Sinnott, eds. *The Battered Elder
  Syndrome: An exploratory study*, unpublished ms.,
  University of Maryland Center on Aging.
Bookin, C. and R.E. Dunkle. 'Elder Abuse: Issues for the
  practitioner,' *Social Casework*, 1985, 66: 3-12
Bragg, D.F., L.R. Kimsey, and A.R. Tarbox. 'Abuse of the
  Elderly - The Hidden Agenda. II. Future Research and
  Remediation,' *Journal of the American Geriatrics Society*,
  1981, 29: 503-7
Burston, G.R. 'Granny Battering,' *British Medical Journal*,
  1975, 3: 592
Champlin, L. 'The Battered Elderly,' *Geriatrics*, 1982,
  37(7): 115-21
Doty, P. and E.W. Sullivan. 'Community Involvement in
  Combating Abuse, Neglect, and Mistreatment in Nursing
  Homes,' *Milbank Memorial Fund Quarterly/Health & Society*,
  1983, 61: 222-51
Douglass, R.L. 'Domestic Neglect and Abuse of the Elderly:
  Implications for Research and Service,' *Family Relations*,
  1983, 32: 395-402
Douglass, R.L., T. Hickey, and C. Noel. *A Study of
  Maltreatment of the Elderly and Other Vulnerable Adults*,
  1980. Ann Arbor: University of Michigan, Institute of
  Gerontology.
Edwards, C. *Elder Abuse - The Hidden Phenomenon*, 1985.
  Ottawa: Health and Welfare Canada. National Clearinghouse
  on Family Violence.
Falcioni, D. 'Assessing the Abused Elderly,' *Journal of
  Gerontological Nursing*, 1982, 8: 208-12
Farrar, M.S. 'Mother-daughter Conflicts Extended into Later
  Life,' *Social Casework*, 1955, 36: 202-7
Faulkner, L. 'Mandating the Reporting of Suspected Cases of
  Elder Abuse: An Inappropriate, Ineffective and Ageist
  Response to the Abuse of Older Adults,' *Family Law
  Quarterly*, 1982, 16: 69-92
Giordano, N.H. and J.A. Giordano. 'Elder Abuse: A Review of
  the Literature,' *Social Work*, 1984, 29: 232-6
Goldstein, S. and A. Blank. 'Editorial: The Elderly: Abused

or Abusers?' *Canadian Medical Association Journal*, 1982, 127: 455-6

Halamandaris, V.J. 'Fraud and Abuse in Nursing Homes,' in J.I. Kosberg, ed. *Abuse and Maltreatment of the Elderly: Causes and Interventions*, 1983, pp. 104-14. Boston: John Wright.

Harvey, R. 'Calls Growing for Big Reforms in Nursing Homes,' *The Toronto Star*, pp. A1, A19, 4 November 1985.

------. 'Sick and Frail Often Feel Neglected, Lonely,' *The Toronto Star*, pp. A1, A12, 5 November 1985.

------. 'Safeguards Urged to Ensure Quality Care,' *The Toronto Star*, pp. A1, A23, 6 November 1985.

Health and Welfare Canada. National Clearninghouse on Family Violence. 'Frail and Vulnerable: Elder Abuse in Canada,' *Vis-a-vis*, 1983, autumn, 1(2): 1-3

Hickey, T. and R.L. Douglass. 'Neglect and Abuse of Older Family Members: Professionals' Perspectives and Case Experiences,' *The Gerontologist*, 1979, 19: 398-402

Hooyman, N.R. 'Mobilizing Social Networks to Prevent Elderly Abuse,' *Physical & Occupational Therapy in Geriatrics*, 1982, 2(2): 21-35

Kalish, R.A. 'The New Ageism and the Failure Models: A Polemic,' *The Gerontologist*, 1979, 19: 398-402

Kimsey, L.R., A.R. Tarbox, and D.F. Bragg. 'Abuse of the Elderly — The Hidden Agenda. I. The Caretakers and the Categories of Abuse,' *Journal of the American Geriatrics Society*, 1981, 29: 465-472

Langley, A. *Abuse of the Elderly* (Human Services Monograph Series). Washington, D.C.: U.S. Government Printing Office.

Lau, E.E. and J.I. Kosberg. 'Abuse of the Elderly by Informal Care Providers,' *Aging*, 1979a, Sept.-Oct., pp. 10-15

------. Editorial. *Journal of the American Medical Association*, 1979b, 241: 18

Legal Research and Services for the Elderly (1979). 'Elder Abuse in Massachusetts: A Survey of Professionals and Paraprofessionals,' unpublished ms. Boston: Author.

Levine, C. 'Intrafamilial Abuse of Elders,' unpublished ms.

O'Malley, T.A., D.E. Everitt, H.C. O'Malley, and E.W. Campion. 'Identifying and Prevening Family-Mediated Abuse and Neglect of Elderly Persons,' *Annals of Internal Medicine*, 1983, 98: 998-1005

O'Rourke, M. 'Elder Abuse: The State of the Art,' paper prepared for the National Conference on the Abuse of Older Persons, Boston.

Pedrick-Cornell, C. and R.J. Gelles. 'Elder Abuse: The
    Status of Current Knowledge,' *Family Relations*, 1982,
    31: 457-65
Podnieks, E. 'Abuse of the Elderly,' *The Canadian Nurse*,
    1983, May, 79: 34-5
Pratt, C.C., J. Koval and S. Lloyd. 'Service Workers'
    Responses to Abuse of the Elderly,' *Social Casework*,
    1983, 64: 147-53
Rathbone-McCuan, E. 'Elderly Victims of Family Violence and
    Neglect,' *Social Casework*, 1980, 61: 296-304
Rose, A. 'Social Welfare in the Canadian Content,' lecture
    notes. University of Toronto.
Shell, D.J. *Protection of the Elderly: A Study of Elder
    Abuse*, 1982. Winnipeg: Manitoba Council on Aging.
Schlesinger, B. 'Elderly Abuse: The Fourth Horsemen,' *The
    Journal*, 1985, 29(5): 13-16
Schlesinger, R.A. 'Granny-bashing: An Introduction to the
    Problem,' *Canadian Women Studies*, 1984, 5(3): 56-9
Solomon, K. 'Victimization by Health Professionals and the
    Psychologic Response of the Elderly,' in J.I. Kosberg,
    ed. *Abuse and Maltreatment of the Elderly: Causes and
    Interventions*, 1983, pp. 150-71. Boston: John Wright.
Steinmetz, S.K. 'Battered Parents,' *Society*, 1978, July-
    August, 15: 54-5
Steuer, J. and E. Austin. 'Family Abuse of the Elderly,'
    Journal of the American Geriatrics Society, 1980,
    28: 372-6
Tarbox, A.R. 'The Elderly in Nursing Homes: Psychological
    Aspects of Neglect,' *Clinical Gerontologist*, 1983,
    1(4): 39-42
Tomita, S.K. 'Detection and Treatment of Elderly Abuse and
    Neglect: A Protocol for Health Care Professional,'
    Physical & Occupational Theray in Geriatrics, 1982, 2(2),
    37-51
Vadasz, M. *Family Abuse of the Elderly*, 1985. Vancouver
    Health Department: distributed by Health and Welfare
    Canada, National Clearinghouse on Family Violence.
Vieno, E.C. 'Victimology: An Overview,' in J.I. Kosberg,
    ed. *Abuse and Maltreatment of the Elderly:
    Causes and Interventions*, 1983, pp. 1-18. Boston: John
    Wright.

Reprinted with permission of the programme in Gerontology,
University of Toronto, Director: Blossom T. Wigdor

3
ELDER ABUSE: IT'S TIME WE DID SOMETHING ABOUT IT
ELIZABETH PODNIEKS

> I pushed her. I know I shouldn't have but I'd had a bad
> day and she knocked her false teeth off the shelf.
> (Nurses aid)

> I don't want to go (into the nursing home) but my
> daughter says if I don't sell the house and give her the
> money she won't have anything to do with me any more.
> (elderly patient)[1]

Elder abuse takes many forms. Sometimes, but not always, it
involves physical cruelty. Sometimes family members are at
fault. Sometimes it is caregivers. The problem is not new:
gerontologists have known about it for years but recognition
among the general public is just beginning to surface. Many
of us would rather not think about the fact that the elderly
among us are vulnerable, that in our own community there are
people who need protection from family members or professional
caregivers.

What drives a person to violence, particularly against
someone he loves, or has loved, someone who trusts him or
has trusted him? Why does love turn into hate and neglect?
What tensions exist within families that such feelings of
brutality are so near the surface? How can we as nurses be
gentle and caring with our own mothers and grandmothers and
then go to work and be impatient and careless with someone
else's loved ones?

The causes of elder abuse are not well understood; research points to a strong correlation betwen dependency,
disability and abuse. Most caregivers are able to cope but
some succumb to the unending burden of the caregiving role
and express their stress in a violent way. Usually a

combination of factors interacts to precipitate abuse:
familial, social/environmental and pathological factors.

Hocking[2], a consultant geriatrician, has found that
people who keep things bottled up are more likely to become
violent. Could this not apply to a caretaker in the home, or
a staff member in an institution? Both, feeling frustration
and weariness, can so easily one day 'let go' and vent all
those pent-up feelings on the elder person who is a captive
victim.

Individuals have differing perceptions and a variety of
ways of defining violence. Bookin[3]'in a recent paper cites
an example of a social worker and her supervisor not being
able to agree on whether a particular case was actually an
abusive situation (the caregiver hitting the elder with a
hair brush in order to control her). The picture became much
clearer when, at the agency's annual family outing, the
supervisor noted the worker physically disciplining her own
child in public. The supervisor realized that she and the
case worker had totally different notions concerning the use
of force. We must carefully examine our attitudes and not be
guilty of imposing our own biases on clients-at-risk.

Whether the caregiver is a tired, guilt-ridden family
member or an overworked, underappreciated nurse, the stress,
isolation and intolerable strain are similar. Eastman[4], a
geriatric social worker, asked one of his clients if she
ever felt like hitting the dependent person in her care and
received the following response: 'Thank God you've asked me
that question. Yes, sometimes, I feel I could knock him
sideways.' Is there a message her for all of us? Would it be
total heresy to say to a nurse, 'Do you sometimes feel like
hitting your client?' Will nurses ever feel secure enough,
comfortable enough, honest enough to admit to themselves and
to their peers some of their real feelings and anxieties
about the caregiving role? How can we get across to caregivers that it's okay to feel anger, frustration, hostility?
It is *not* okay to express these feelings in a way that
threatens the recipients of our care.

We must learn to recognize stress signals and get help
before these feelings are transferred to abusive behavior.[5]

The elderly refuse to report abuse: they are mortified by
the situation. They have many fears: loss of love, retaliation, relocation. Nurses too have great difficulty in reporting 'miscare.' We must take every effort to support our
colleagues but let there be no misunderstanding: nurses

don't have any option in the reporting of elder abuse. Even if the abuser is our best friend or the head nurse, we have an ethical responsibility defined by the standards established by the Canadian Nurses Association.

Documentation of elder abuse has increased significantly in the past few years. Nevertheless, accessing the mistreated elderly remains a major problem. Health care professionals often ignore or overlook the possibility of non-accidental injury and have not learned to recognize the signs and precipitating factors which can place the elderly in potentially abusive situations.[6] Studies have shown that abusers often *do* ask for help - only to find that no one is listening.

> I am afraid I will lose control of myself, I might even murder her ... I consulted my G.P., my minister, the district nurse, social worker and friends. No one seems able to help me ...[7]

If anyone can reach the neglected or abused elderly, it is the nurse. The nursing process has prepared nurses to be particularly perceptive in identifying an elderly client in a crisis situation; the data she collects and her assessment and diagnosis determine the appropriate planning and management.

The initial interview will challenge all of the nurse's resources: she must maximize her observational skills and communication techniques. The abused client, who may have been living with pain and guilt for years, is anxious, probably ashamed, definitely afraid. The nurse must be watching for any cue or indication of stress in either the client or the accompanying caregiver. Collecting data from an elderly person is not easy: it requires patience, tact, discretion and above all a capacity to engender trust. How many of us would be willing to disclose information so embarrassing, so personal as the abusive behaviour of the caregiver on whom we are dependent? We must be prepared to ask sensitive questions. We haven't been too embarrased to ask our clients about their sexuality; now we must ask them how they really broke that arm, where did those bruises come from, why are they afraid?

Never make a nursing diagnosis of elder abuse until all assessments have been completed - history, physical and psychological examinations. Remember that sometimes the signs of physical abuse are actually due to the aging process.[8] Similarly, signs of psychological abuse may be due to social, cultural or other factors.[9]

Fundamental to the intervention phase of the nursing process is the nurse's comprehensive knowledge of social supports and community resources. She cannot and must not intervene alone: she is part of a multidisciplinary team of coordinated workers. Intervention must include treatment modalities for the abuser as well as for the victim.

Intervention strategies require a continuum of care whereby the elderly person can move from one type of help to another as his health status changes. The ultimate goal of the continuum of care is to provide an active and fulfilling life in later years. A full range of home care and respite services includes: medical and legal assistance, visiting nurses, homemakers, home repair, friendly visiting, adult day care, respite care, physical and occupational therapy, nutrition services, telephone checking systems, transportation, emergency shelters, counselling and education, as well as providing assistance in learning problem-solving skills. Other interventions are: informal support systems (family, friends, neighbours, peers); local community organizatons; gatekeepers (eg., postal workers, delivery people, public utility workers); self-help groups, volunteers and resident counsels. These community-based supports are essential if elders are to remain in their own homes.

As practitioners, what can we do to become change agents in the social phenomenon of elder abuse? First, we can recognize the problem. We can be more sensitive to the dilemma facing those in the caretaking role. We can be aware of the diversity of social factors which precipitate violence. We can gain an understanding of how caregivers might react by being more aware of the methods *we* use to cope with stress and frustration.[10]

We can think about the loneliness and isolation of the elderly person who is faced with loss of control and privacy. We can educate professionals and the public to detect and report abuse. We can foster the self-esteem and self-worth of all elderly persons, reverse the 'learned helplessness' and 'learned violence' that is transmitted from one generation to the next. We can lobby for legislation that will ensure the protection of elders, while acknowledging the importance of preserving the older person's autonomy.

36 Elizabeth Podnieks

References

1. *Globe and Mail*, Toronto. 10 Feb. 1985.
2. Hocking, E.M. 'Granny Battering,' by S. Edwards, *Medical News*, Nov. 1982.
3. Bookin, Deborah. 'Elder Abuse: Issue for the Practioner.' Paper presented at the Gerontological Society of America, San Francisco, Nov. 1983: 9.
4. Eastman, M. 'The Battering of Mrs. Scaffle,' *New Age*, 1981.
5. Podnieks, E. 'Elder Abuse.' Paper presented at the Second National Conference on Gerontological Nursing, Winnipeg, Manitoba, 22 May 1984.
6. Hooyman, Nancy, and Sue Tomita. 'Interventions in Cases of Elderly Abuse Within Medical Settings.' Paper presented at the Annual Meeting of the Western Gerontological Society, San Diego, March 1982.
7. Eastman, M. 'Elder Abuse,' *Age Concern*, 1984.
8. Humphreys, J., J. Campbell, and S. Barrett. 'Clinical Intervention with the Abused Elderly and Their Families.' Paper presented at the Gerontological Society of America, San Francisco, Nov. 1983.
9. Eastman, M. 'Elder Abuse,' *Age Concern*, 1984.
10. Parkin, M.W. 'Domestic Violence Against Women, *Australian Nurses Journal*, Vol. 12, No. 4, Oct. 1982.

Reproduced with permission from *The Canadian Nurse*, Vol. 81, No. 11, pp. 36-39.

Accessing the mistreated elderly: indicators of abuse

Definition of Abuse

Any act or behavior by a family member or person providing care (formally or informally) which results in physical or mental harm or neglect of an elderly person. This would include but is not necessarily confined to the following examples:

Physical Abuse   Willful, direct infliction of physical pain or injury. Denial or physical and health related necessities of life.

Neglect   Lack of attention, abandonment, and confinement of the elderly by family members or society.

Psychosocial Abuse   Removal of decision-making power from the elderly. Withholding of affection, social isolation.

Exploitation   Any situation involving the dishonest use of an elderly person's resources, such as money or property. Misappropriation of health care resources.

Profile of Elder Abuse Victim	Profile of Abuser
■ over age 75 ■ female/widow/single ■ progressive physical and/or mental impairment ■ denies abuse: reluctant to report ■ increasingly dependent on abuser for physical/emotional needs ■ socially isolated ■ may feel abuse is deserved	■ middle aged ■ family member/caregiver ■ experiencing stress: financial problems, medical problems, marital conflict, substance abuse unemployment ■ increasing demands of caregiving role depleting family resources ■ resents role reversal with parent ■ ineffective coping patterns ■ ineffective communication patterns

Categories of Abuse and Neglect	

Physical Abuse	Indicators
■ assault, beating, cutting, burning, forced feeding, hitting, slapping, pinching, punching, pushing, pulling hair, shaking, shoving	■ unexplained alopecia, abrasions, bruises, burns, bumps, contusions, falls, fractures, grip marks, hematomas, immobility, infections, internal injuries, lacerations, pain, restricted movement, rope marks, swelling, tenderness, ulcers, welts
■ sexual molestation ■ rape ■ hypo/hyperthermia	■ pain, bruising, bleeding in genital area ■ shivering, cyanosis, flushed, lowered/elevated body temperature
■ homicide	

Neglect	Indicators
■ withholding nutrition, fluids	■ malnourished, emaciated, no dentures, dehydration, mouth sores, confusion
■ inadequate hygiene, personal care	■ impaired skin integrity, decubitus ulcers, rashes, urine burns, soiled linen, unkempt appearance
■ inadequate clothing	■ clothes in poor repair, inappropriate for season
■ overmedicated — drugs, alcohol	■ oversedation — reduced physical/mental activity ■ CNS depression
■ undermedicated	■ reduced/absent therapeutic response
■ sensory deprivation ■ lack of safety precautions ■ lack of supervision ■ withholding medical services/treatment ■ unjustified use of restraints	■ no glasses, hearing aid ■ dangerous environment ■ unattended, tied to chair/bed ■ not taken to doctor/dentist/therapist ■ muscle contractures, immobility, weakness
■ abandonment ■ forced entry into nursing home	■ deserted ■ institutionalized

Psychosocial Abuse	Indicators
■ humiliation ■ dehumanization ■ intimidation ■ non-verbal abuse/silence ■ provoking fear ■ verbal abuse — shouting, scolding ■ imposed social isolation ■ withholding of companionship/love ■ lack of privacy ■ removal of decision-making process ■ infantilization ■ threats of abandonment, institutionalization, physical abuse, withdrawal of love	■ appears shamed ■ low self-esteem ■ withdrawn, passive ■ fearful, "what are you going to do to me?" ■ invalid guilt ■ excluded from family gatherings, not permitted to have friends visit, to go to church, denied access to grandchildren ■ embarrassment ■ loss of self determination ■ ribbons in hair, toys, "baby talk" ■ depressed, hopeless, helpless
Exploitation	**Indicators**
■ inequitable distribution of health care resources ■ fraud, misuse of elder's money/property ■ coercion ■ resource abuse ■ withholding pensions/insurance cheque ■ theft	■ medical underdiagnosis/under-treatment ■ inappropriate hospital discharge ■ inappropriate transfer within institution ■ nursing attitudes — lack of understanding, custodialism, paternalism ■ inadequate community supports ■ overcharged for home repairs, funerals ■ "con artists" ■ illegal use of elder's possessions/property/investments for profit/personal gain ■ abuser supports own drug/alcohol dependency ■ forced to sign over control/power of attorney ■ forced to change will, sell house ■ used as baby sitter/housekeeper ■ no money for food/clothes ■ inadequate living environment ■ unable to afford social activities, travel ■ disappearance of elder's possessions in institutions

Observations Which Trigger Further Assessment

Presenting Behavior of Elder

- has physical/mental limitations affecting self-care ability
- medical history does not coincide with presenting injuries
- postpones seeking medical treatment
  has sores, injuries which have not been treated/partially healed
- history shows repeated incidents of unexplained "accidents"/injuries
- gives history of seeking medical attention from a variety of doctors/treatment centres
- gives information reluctantly: waits for caregiver to supply answers
- avoids physical, verbal contact with caregiver/professional

Cognitive Responses of Elder

- affect, emotion: agitated, anxious, dejected, depressed, excited, fearful, flat, humiliated, overly quiet, resigned, unresponsive
- speech: hesitant, inaudible, loud, rapid, slow
- nonverbal behavior: cringing, hands clenched, rigid, rocking, passive, avoids facial, eye contact with caregiver/professional

Presenting Behavior of Caregiver

- refuses to permit hospitalization/diagnostic tests
- ignores elder's hospital admission — doesn't visit
- may refuse to participate in discharge planning or take elder home
- impatient with staff/procedures
- appears fatigued, stressed
- "blames" elder
- responds defensively when questioned: makes excuses, hostile, suspicious, irritable, demanding
- does not want elder interviewed alone

Caregiver Behavior Toward Elder

- excessively concerned/unconcerned
- treats elder like a child or non person
- has minimal eye, facial, physical, verbal contact with elder

High Risk Factors Which Precipitate Elder ABuse	

Familial	Societal/Environmental
■ caregiver lack of knowledge of aging process and caregiving duties: services and resources available, how to access them ■ psychological, physical impairments in elderly ■ age/psychological/physical health of caregiver ■ caregiver stress ■ caregiver pressured into caretaking role: guilt, financial reasons ■ caregiver has other dependents ■ poor family inter-relationships ■ multiple family problems ■ elder experiencing recent meaningful losses: bereavement, loss of independence, mobility ■ social isolation of caregiver and elder, lack of social and emotional support network ■ family history of violence ■ caregiver has poor impulse control ■ unreasonable expectations of capabilities of elder by caregiver or vice versa ■ substance abuse of elder or caregiver ■ altered lifestyle of caregiver ■ fewer available caregivers due to disappearance of nuclear family, ie: one-parent families ■ caregiver's refusal to accept, or fear of, own aging ■ role fatigue, changing roles, role dissatisfaction ■ learned helplessness of elderly ■ refusal of elder and/or caregiver to accept help	■ lack of societal concern for elderly ■ lack of understanding of aging process ■ stereotyping of elderly, ageism ■ inadequate resources — social services, social planning, community support ■ poverty of women, financial stress, lack of reimbursement for caring for elderly at home ■ inadequate housing, overcrowding ■ unemployment of caregiver ■ fear of crime, inadequate safety measures in environment ■ lack of alternatives for elder other than institutionalization ■ lack of uniform definition of abuse ■ lack of professional awareness of abuse problem — lack of detection/reporting protocols ■ lack of legislation dealing with rights of elderly

	Institutional
	■ poor working environment ■ inadequate preparation of staff ■ lack of opportunity for staff professional/personal growth ■ increasing dependency of elderly, extreme impairments ■ lack of understanding of aging process, complex health needs of elderly ■ negative attitude toward aging ■ insensitivity to needs of elderly and families ■ lack of positive communication between staff/clients/families ■ lack of legislation and policies to ensure quality care in institutions ■ insufficient number of caregivers ■ insufficient number of registered nurses

INTERVENTION

Primary Prevention

- **legislation:** to establish legislative measures and policies which will protect the rights of elderly persons
  to provide health and social services which will maintain the independence of the elderly within the community or care facility

- **advocacy:** to represent the views of the elderly
  to articulate their special needs
  to foster an appreciation of the developmental stage of the elderly

- **research:** to determine the causes leading to abuse
  to develop a valid and reliable assessment tool

- **education:** to increase public and professional awareness of the abuse problem
  to further understanding of the aging process

Secondary Prevention

- establishment of screening programs for elder abuse
- medical intervention for treatment of injuries; treatment of abuser
- develop plan of intervention to address elder abuse
- provision of protective services/legal intervention/guardianship
- coordination of community support system to ensure quality continuum care. Stress reducing measures through informal supports, networking, peer counselling and appropriate formal services
- family therapy involving elder, abuser, other family members
- educational programs to teach effective caregiving roles using a problem-solving process

Tertiary Prevention

- rehabilitation, assisting the elder to achieve his/her optimum level of health and safety, may involve permanent change to create a more supportive environment
- rehabilitation of abuser — ongoing counselling, group support

4
ELDER ABUSE AND ITS IMPACT ON HOSPITAL SOCIAL WORK
PAUL GIRARD

Introduction

Adult protection services since the early 1960's have been too limited and have not been designed to deal with the basic cause of elder abuse and neglect. Staudt (1985) concludes that there are four commonalities either implicitly or explicitly stated in definitions of adult protective service. Usually these commonalities (adult protective services) can be defined as that network of services - social, medical, legal, or other - provided to adults who (1) are in danger of harm or are harming others; (2) are not capable of taking action in their own behalf; (3) have no significant others available or willing to provide assistance; and (4) have their decision-making power designated to another - a situation which would involve the use of legal intervention.

These criterion are obviously too vague and, therefore, difficult to apply. The area of elder abuse is a very serious one considering that a social worker must challenge both the competency of an individual to look after himself and then accuse a family member or caregiver of having motivations that are not in the best interest of the patient. A social worker must be prepared to confront caregivers saying that they do not have the ability to give care or that their concern for the elder is secondary to the financial rewards of looking after the patient. Needless to say a caregiver's reaction to such statements will be anything from relief to rage. The social worker must be zealous and concerned. He must have confidence that he is right, after reviewing the facts, and must be interested in providing safety to the elder no matter what the person's prognosis. Staudt (1985) suggests that adult protection services have been sporadic in their development because of a lack of knowledge and even a lack of interest.

The extent of the problem

There are two schools of thought about the extent of the problem of elder abuse. The first is that to abuse or neglect an incompetent old person is a despicable act and, therefore, a rare event. The second line of thinking is that when people get motivated by money or similar advantages (e.g., free housing), the care of the elder becomes secondary and taking advantage of the monies accruing to the elder is primary. Zborowsky (1985) points out that the number of older people vulnerable to abuse, neglect and exploitation has continued to grow along with the general increase in the United States' population aged 65 and older. Regan (1977) estimated that between 10 and 15 per cent, or 3 to 4 million elderly persons, are in need of protective services.

In applying these estimates to Canada, up to 400,000 elders across this nation could be in need of adult protection services and, as of this date (July 1985), only New Brunswick has specific protection services. The situation in Canada may even be worse. The incidence of elder abuse may be much higher than previously suspected because of Canada's system of universal social programs for seniors and the automation of the delivery of the benefits. Again, this suspicion comes from the American experience.

Hall (1971) set the stage. The Social Security Administration, the Veteran's Administration, and the American Public Welfare Association were confronted with an increased number of recipients of retirement and old age assistance benefits who evidenced serious difficulties in handling their cheques. Most of these older people did not require psychiatric hospitalization. At the same time, it was usually not possible for them to pay the fees for a court-appointed guardian to help them manage their affairs in the community. The three agencies eventually dealt with the problem by establishing procedures for making a relative or other interested person the 'representative payee' for the older person's cheque. Despite various safeguards, the representative payee procedure has been used to exploit some older people.

The solution backfired and, in fact, compounded the problem. In Canada there are only routine banking safeguards and there are virtually no monitoring devices to discourage a self-appointed representative payee from financially exploiting a marginally competent older person. Well-automated efficient universal welfare schemes may be con-

tributing significantly to an increase in opportunities for
elder neglect and financial exploitation to exist.

The statement of the problem

With the development of any type of protection services, be
it children's protection or adult protection, the populations being served are seen to be dependent on a competent
person to provide at least the basic needs. However, in
comparing the two populations (the child and the elder),
differences and similarities become apparent.

The obvious similarity in the populations who inflict the
abuse or withhold the basic needs on a repeated basis is
that they are likely to be alcoholic or be in the process of
becoming alcoholic and/or drug dependent. The fact always
seems to be evident in any type of abuse situation but is
rarely addressed, rarely seen as primary. This is usually
seen as a secondary element that results from being in a
'stressed' situation. It is a factor that is usually
recognized then ignored.

Children more than elders are able to arouse the col-
lective conscience of a community. There is an opportunity
cost for the elder in that a society will more readily give
attention and resources to children and not focus interest,
concern or resources on the elders. When it comes to
children, given the proper course of treatment and care,
they can overcome the scars of abuse and can have positive
productive futures. In the case of elders, rehabilitation
over an extended period of time is not likely and, in many
cases of elder abuse conditions worsen over time and the
outcome is death. Given this lack of opportunity to provide
treatment and have positive outcomes, some are of the
opinion, at least covertly, - why bother? Further, when you
realize that the events (the abuse and neglect over a period
of time) that precede a death can be directly connected to
the death, social workers (along with other health professionals) will tend to shy away because now they must get
involved after-the-fact with a very serious criminal charge.
Even police have been known to make very superficial investigations of alleged abuse cases because no interested
people are around who are still concerned about the person
who died.

The most significant difference between children and
elders is that abuse of children seems to be motivated out
of rage, frustration, a sense of the children being a burden

or being unwanted. The root of the motivation seems to be
emotional or psychological. The roots of the motivation for
elder abuse and neglect seem to be financial. Girard (1984)
hypothesized that the motivating factor which underlines all
cases of extended elder abuse and neglect is that the perpetrator realizes or believes that there is some quantifi-
able monetary gain (in cash or in kind) either on an ongoing
basis or as an outcome of death. The motivation to continu-
ally abuse or neglect an elderly person basically comes from
a cost-benefit decision. The abuser is either betting that
the estate of the elder will outlast the elder or that ongoing universal pension, retirement payments, dividend
cheques or housing will be greater than the cost of caring
for the elder.

The interveners

In the fall of 1983, a survey was done by the instructor of
a Social Services Course sponsored by the Department of
Social Services of Nova Scotia. Haley (1983) drew the focus
on elder abuse by describing the phenomenon. He then called
together a multidisciplinary group of professionals to act
more or less as a lobby group to actively address the problem. The group had representation from hospital social work,
medicine, nursing, community nursing, as well as from the
Department of Social Services and the Senior Citizens'
Directorate. I, as the representative of the Victoria
General Hospital, then had the opportunity to write a paper
on the topic and present it locally. Each member of the
lobby group set out simply to do that - lobby. The government of the day, as represented by Honourable Edmund Morris,
was apparently listening and responsive and drew up Bill
No. 61. The whole process took only about one year. The
outcome was the new adult protection act and a reinforcing
of another related act.

The laws - the tools

On 17 May 1985 the Nova Scotia government assented to Bill
No. 61, an Act to Provide for Protection of Adults from
Abuse and Neglect. The Act was proclaimed in the fall of
1985 and, with it, a structure to deliver the protection
services. Nova Scotia is the second Canadian province to
have such a service. The purpose of the Act is to provide a
means whereby adults who lack the ability to care and fend

adequately for themselves can be protected from abuse and
neglect by providing them with access to services which will
enhance their ability to care and fend for themselves or
which will protect them from abuse or neglect.

Basically the Act describes abuse and neglect as the
presenting problem; that is, to safeguard the dependent
adult from being abused or neglected. The Act takes one more
important step by making reference to the role of the Public
Trustee. It is this reference by which the Act implicitly
accepts the premise that abuse and neglect are motivated by
financial exploitation. The Public Trustee can be referred
cases in which he can assume immediate management of the
estate of a person suspected of being abused. Intervention
by the Public Trustee is appropriate when there are reasonable and probable grounds for believing that a patient is
the victim of physical abuse or breach of trust by a person
claiming to have lawful control over the patient, or over
the patient's estate, by virtue of Power of Attorney,
Instrument of Trust or Court Order.

In the case of incompetency, the Public Trustee can
become the patient's 'legal' guardian and make decisions
relative to his care. However, this only happens when no
other viable alternatives are available.

Given that the premise is true about the motivating
factor being money, it is likely that, in the future, the
matter of elder abuse and neglect will be a rather rare
event for the police or criminal justice system, but rather
a banal issue for the Public Trustee. The new Act will
increase the workload of the Public Trustee and hopefully
the office will remain responsive by increasing its major
resource - staff.

Like most child protection legislation, there is a clause
requiring mandatory reporting. The Act states that every
person who has information, whether or not it is confiden-
tial or privileged, indicating that an adult is in need of
protection shall report information to the Minister. This
clause now gives the hospital social worker somewhere to go
to begin the process of offering protection to the patient.
It acts as a starting point by which allegations can be investigated and action taken if proven accurate. The only requirement for reporting is that there is an honest suspicion
that abuse or neglect is occurring. The social worker does
not have the onus of providing the case, just reporting it.

In summary, what the Act does for the hospital social
worker is provide an opportunity to report a case of abuse

or neglect, gives assurance that the matter will be
investigated, and provides a direct link to the Public
trustee to ensure that more long-term protection can be
provided.

The role of the hospital social worker

Before the establishment of the Adult Protection Legislation
and before the Public Trustee's Act was strengthened, the
role of the hospital social worker was very frustrating when
a case of abuse or neglect was identified because very
little could be done. The incompetent abused elders would
not be able to describe their circumstance, could not
comprehend the alternatives and didn't know that they had
rights. They would elect to return home to the abusing
situation because, if alert, they felt old, feeble and
inadequate, they felt that anyone else would also see them
as a burden. Therefore, they would simply reiterate the
statements made by the abuser, say there was nothing wrong
and go home – only to return in the near future.

If the social worker was able to get into a position of
confronting the perpetrator, he would be put in the position
of proving the accusations. The perpetrator would, in turn,
say things like, 'I am her closest relative and she gets so
lonely', or 'she made me promise her I would not put her in
a home'. or 'she's my mother who looked after me, now it's
my turn.' In lieu of an investigation these bleeding-heart
statements would have to be accepted.

With such negative outcomes it would hardly be worthwhile
to even try to recognize the problem. If you cannot do anything except get frustrated when you recognize the problem,
eventually you learn not to look for it. When you stumbled
upon it, you would try to deny it and wind up accepting the
incongruent statements of the abuser. With the legislation
in place, the role of the social worker is critical. The
social worker must first learn how to see the problem, gain
the co-operation of the health care team, and then use the
resources available to carry out effective discharge
planning.

In hospital an old person will present a physical problem
related to abuse or neglect. There may be evidence of unexplained bruising or fractures typical in any assault victim,
but more than likely there will be evidence of neglect; that
is, there will be gross hygiene problems. The patient may
also show problems related to poor nutritional intake, i.e.,

dehydration and starvation. Finally, the patient may appear
drugged or over-medicated. Obviously, at this point financial exploitation will never be seen as the presenting problem, but rather can be looked for to confirm the diagnosis
of abuse/neglect.

Once abuse or neglect is suspected, the social worker
must begin an investigation. (In this case the best term for
what the social worker is doing is 'investigating' rather
than assessing.) Since abuse is a patterned or re-occurring
problem, there may be previous admissions at the hospital or
other hospitals in the community. Agencies like V.O.N., Red
Cross or Community Nursing may have had some contact in the
past, and finally the family doctor should be contacted to
try to get his input. In talking to the agencies and
doctors, the social worker will usually hear frustrating
stories of aborted attempts to help - stories of failure.

Many surveys have been done in the United States to find
out what exactly are the high risk factors related to elder
abuse/neglect. The results have been non-conclusive and
highly speculative.

From the literature Zborowsky (1985) suggests some
tentative patterns in the problem of elder abuse. White
females, aged 80 and older, with a major physical or mental
disability that prevented them from meeting their own daily
needs seemed to be at greater risk for abuse. They tended to
live with others and in the same household as their abusers.
The abusers were most often adult children; less than 20 per
cent of the reported abuse was inflicted by a non-relative.
Earlier Ferguson (1978) as a result of protective service
research and demonstration projects provided descriptive
information about their respective clients. He suggests that
clients tended to be aged 75 or older, females, white, and
currently not married. Further, they usually lived in a
private house or apartment and were not destitute relative
to national income standards.

The Victoria General Hospital's experience with elder
abuse confirms these general profiles. Further to this, in
all cases the victims have owned their own homes, all were
being exploited by the perpetrators by having their
Guaranteed Income Supplement and Old Age Security cheques
cashed without benefit and in all cases alcoholism in the
perpetrator was either prevalent or at least suspected, if
not confirmed.

The perpetrators usually are relatives, and usually a son
or daughter; they are alcoholic or drug dependent, have been

subject to abuse themselves, talk about handling things in a physical manner and are inclined to look for revenge. They are usually unemployed and live in the home of the elder and may live with a spouse, girlfriend (boyfriend) or friends.

There have been no single cases of physical abuse without neglect; with physical abuse there is further evidence of neglect. However, in most cases neglect is the presenting problem. When asked to explain the neglected state of the patient, the abuser's statements are usually incongruent to the actual facts. No matter how good the story, it cannot explain the extreme state of some patients. In order to distract the investigator, the perpetrator will offer pious platitudes about how special the relationship is between the patient and themselves.

Therefore in order for neglect to occur the elder person:

(a) must be vulnerable either because of physical or mental limitation;
(b) must have assets that are accessible (usually housing, money, or both); and
(c) the perpetrator must be in need of benefits or think he has no alternatives.

There must be opportunity, motivation and benefits if the crime is to exist. Because this is investigated like a crime, the social worker must learn to develop with a 'high index of suspicion.'

Once there is enough evidence to suspect neglect or abuse, the social worker must register the case and present it to the adult protection agency for further investigation or confirmation.

In the majority of cases, the estate of the patient is critical in that, if it is no longer accessible to the perpetrator, the motivation is gone and the abuser will yield quickly. Therefore, the case (at this point the estate) of the patient is referred to the Public Trustee and, if necessary, he can immediately take over the responsibility of the estate.

If the patient is incompetent, a referral must be made to psychiatry to confirm this with a specific diagnosis. When a patient is incompetent, the Public Trustee is then responsible for the guardianship of the patient and will remain directly responsible if there is no suitable available next-of-kin. When the patient is competent, she is encouraged to

keep her estate in trust, that is, administered by the
Public Trustee and advised of alternatives available, e.g.,
nursing home placement or comprehensive home care program.

Finally the process of discharge planning will result in
placement into a nursing home; and in Nova Scotia this
usually means that a referral is made to the municipality of
settlement for immediate or imminent financial assistance
and to the province for classification. Then the last problem is to find a nursing home bed.

In summary, there are legal tools used to assist the
social worker in the discharge planning process:

1. *The Act to Provide Protection of Adults from Abuse
    and Neglect* - calls for the hospital social worker to
    report the alleged abuse or neglect and gives the
    social worker assurance that the patient's home
    situation will be thoroughly investigated and action
    taken if necessary;

2. *The Incompetent Persons Act* - gives the psychiatrists
    (a member of the health care team) a vehicle to
    declare a vulnerable, non-functioning person to be
    incompetent thus available for guardianship; and

3. *The Public Trustee Act* - the mandate of the Public
    Trustee is to take action on behalf of the patient by
    at least handling the patient's financial affairs
    and, in some cases, being the patient's guardian.

Cases

The presentation of some recent cases will help to show how
elder abuse and neglect are seen in the hospital setting,
what the salient issues are and what outcomes are possible.

Case 1
Ruth K., an 81 year old woman who lived with her son, an
unemployed accountant with a known drinking problem. She was
brought to emergency in a confused mental state and described
as 'dirty, unkept ... excoriated areas under ventral hernia,
urine burns on buttocks ... candida on excoriated areas ...
long dirty fingernails.' The caregiver did not apparently
supervise the patient's diet or ensure the provision of
adequate personal care.

The patient's son admitted to occasionally going away for days at a time and relying on a niece to look in on her during those times. He had rejected any type of community services including V.O.N., which had been initiated after a previous admission in September 1984, after she had lain on the floor at home for two days.

The patient was not declared incompetent but the estate of the person was given over to the Public Trustee, the son was confronted that he could not provide adequate care and Ruth was placed in a nursing home. Her son now visits only when he is sober.

Case 2

May B., a 75 year old woman who lived with her son who presently is on a disability pension, is obese and is an active alcoholic. On admission the patient was described as being very dirty and severely emaciated. It was concluded that she received inadequate care in regard to personal care and nourishment. While in hospital her appetite improved; however, she remained confused and disoriented much of the time. She did insist on returning home.

The son admitted to difficulties in regard to managing his mother at home because of her unwillingness and inability to co-operate. At home he claimed that she had a poor appetite and refused to eat.

The patient was declared incompetent and the trusteeship of the estate was taken from the son and put in the hands of the Public Trustee. The patient was able to convince the discharge planners to place her at home with home supports and V.O.N. visits. However, it appears that the plan is not viable because the son is becoming unco-operative again, actively drinking, and is refusing to allow community supports to come into the home.

Case 3

Joan J. is a 92 year old woman who lived alone for the past 20 years in a rather expensive highrise apartment building in Halifax. Her caregiver was a friend who lived in a nearby apartment. On admission the patient was described as needing a hearing aid, teeth, proper nutrition and clothing. She had infected feet due to neglect of toe nails and corns and was very dirty. The apartment was visited and was seen as dirty, e.g., no soap to wash pots and pans; the stove and kettle were out of order.

Her neighbour had trusteeship of her estate. When asked about the lack of personal needs, she stated that there was a need to save Joan's money ... she also refused services and was unwilling to have people enter the apartment.

The patient was not declared incompetent but trusteeship was taken from the friend. The patient returned to her home situation with a full home support program. It was alleged that in this case the patient's good furniture was taken by the caregiver and that the caregiver was the benefactor of the will.

Case 4

Anna C., an 82 year old woman widowed for several years, lived in her own home with her granddaughter who was described as being mentally slow. The patient came to hospital dehydrated and with bed sores on her coccyx. A V.O.N. report strongly suggested that the patient required far more nursing care than she was getting. (The caregiver requested they come less frequently.) Another relative reported that just eight months prior Anna's sister died of what he believed to be neglect from the same caregiver.

The granddaughter admitted that physically the patient was too heavy to turn, etc., and that she did not want to spend money as she would need money to live. It was alleged that the caregiver would not give the patient food or drink because the patient had no bowel control and she (the caregiver) did not want to clean the messes.

The patient was declared incompetent and referred to the Public Trustee. She was discharged to a nursing home as a private pay patient. In this case the estate was large enough that a trust fund was established for the caregiver and she was allowed to remain in the house.

Case 5

Pearl M., an 83 year old woman, lived with her son in her own home. The son was unemployed and a well known alcoholic who bootlegged from his mother's home. He also had a criminal record that included violent crimes. The patient came to hospital with a black eye, was dehydrated and had bed sores. Once the patient was admitted, other family members stated they felt intimidated by the caregiver and, therefore, never came forth but several other daughters described the home situation as 'unsafe.' The patient, herself, was widowed for several years and was a heavy drinker in the past.

The caregiver explained the black eye by describing his mother as having 'spells' and she often fell down; he described her lack of hygiene and care as a one time thing. After an initial contact, this son did not maintain any further contact. Throughout her hospitalization, the patient remained very confused.

The patient was declared incompetent and the trusteeship of the estate was taken from the son and put in the hands of the Public Trustee. Another more reliable son was given guardianship but found home care too difficult and he is now trying to find a suitable nursing home. The patient's house has been sold and the monies are used for her care. The sale of the house created a housing problem for the original caregiver.

The cases presented do, in fact, confirm the profiles of neglect or abused elders. In all the cases the patient was female, white, widowed and over seventy-five years old. In all cases the presenting problem was related to neglect as evidenced by poor hygiene and nutrition; only in one case was physical abuse even suspected. Further, every case gave an indication that the pattern of neglect was well established and was not, in effect, something that happened once and then corrected. In all cases the patient was mentally limited in that they were confused and incoherent at least on admission.

One question that was not asked but perhaps might be significant is; what kind of medication was the patient on and how was it administered? It is well known that abused adults are overtly or covertly abused by being given too many mood modifying drugs.

In three out of the five cases the caregiver was alcoholic and male; in the other two cases the caregivers were female and one was of limited functional ability (little is known about the friend who was a caregiver as she quickly dissociated herself). In every case there were immediate financial benefits; in all cases security cheques were available to the caregiver; and in four cases free housing was a reward. In all cases the original explanation of the presenting problem was both incomplete and incongruent, but in one case the caregiver did admit to being concerned about her own welfare over that of the patient. In three of the five cases other agencies, primarily the V.O.N., had a concern about frustrating and marginal involvement. Finally, in all cases the trusteeship of the person's estate played a part in the resolution of the problem. It is apparent that a declaration of incompetency will most significantly affect guardianship and trusteeship. In the two cases where the patient returned to a home situation, the outcome was questionable but the referral to nursing home seemed to have more positive outcomes.

Conclusion

The comprehensiveness of the Nova Scotia model seems to approximate the structure proposed to the United States Congress. Regan and Springer (1977) put forth a model that included an adult protective services act; guardianship, conservatorship of property, and power of attorney legislation and a public guardian act. With such a thorough protocol that is able quickly and significantly to alter individuals' and families' life situations, caution and prudence must prevail.

The most profound ethical question was originally raised by Blenkner (1974) when he reported on the Benjamin Rose Institute Study and found that the experimental service (that was similar to the model described here) appeared to increase the chance of death which was associated with a higher rate of institutionalization, used as a protective intervention. The question that must be addressed is whether or not the intervention will improve the quality of life for the individual; and the challenge to the social worker is to be creative in looking for solutions and not always opt for the cookbook solution of institutionalization.

References

Blenkner, M., M. Bloom, M. Nielson, and R. Weber. *Final Report Protective Services for Older People Findings from the Benjamin Rose Institute (Pt. 1)*. Cleveland: Benjamin Rose Institute, 1974.

Ferguson, E.J. *Protecting the Vulnerable Act*. Ann Arbor, Michigan: University of Michigan - Wayne State University, Institute of Gerontology, 1978.

Haley, R. *A Demographic Survey of the Incidents of Elder Abuse in Nova Scotia*. Halifax, Nova Scotia: Report to the Nova Scotia Department of Social Services, 1983.

Hall, G.H. 'Protective Services for Adults,' *Encyclopedia of Social Work* (Vol. 2, 16th issue). New York: National Association of Social Workers, 1971.

Girard, P.H. *The Pay Off for the Elder Abuse*, a paper presented to the Canadian Association of Social Work Administrators in Health Facilities (CASWAHF), St. John's, Nfld., October, 1984.

Regan, J.J. 'Intervention Through Adult Protective Services Programs,' *Gerontologist*, 18 June 1978, p. 250.

Staudt, M. 'The Social Worker as an Advocate in Adult Protection Services,' *Social Work*, Vol. 30, No. 3, June 1985, pp. 204-8.

Zborowsky, E. 'Development in Protective Services: A Challenge for Social Workers,' *Journal of Gerontological Social Work*, Vol. 8, Nos. 3/4, spring/summer, 1985.

Unpublished paper, reproduced with permission of the author.

5
ELDER ABUSE: AN ASSESSMENT TEAM
BETH ISRAEL HOSPITAL ASSESSMENT TEAM[1]

Introduction

Recent awareness of neglect and violence directed toward the
elderly and recognition of elder abuse as a wide-spread
problem are prompting an organized social response. Until
the late 1970s, there had been little in the way of systematic documentation or public recognition of elder abuse.
Walsh's (1977) paper on 'granny bashing' opened the topic in
Great Britain and was followed by a series of studies in the
United States. The Ohio Study (Lau and Kosberg, 1979) provided a descriptive, retrospective chart review of 404 cases.
The Massachusetts Study (O'Malley et al., 1979) surveyed
1,044 professional and paraprofessional care providers. The
Maryland Study (Block and Sinnott, 1979) used a mailed survey
of care professionals in a selected community, and the
Michigan Study (Douglass, 1979) interviewed 228 professionals
in 5 community sites. These studies indicated that those at
greatest risk for abuse are very old (more than 75 years),
female, and dependent on others because of physical or
cognitive impairment.

These preliminary studies, as well as press coverage of
the issue, have led to 'elder abuse' legislation in a majority of states. Most legislative efforts include 'reporting'
laws, which encourage or require professionals or the lay
public to report cases of suspected abuse or neglect. Implementation of such legislation has raised difficult philosoph-
ical and practical questions for professionals and service-
providing institutions which encounter individuals with conditions or injuries that could be caused by abuse or neglect.

The purpose of this paper is to describe the development
and ongoing function of a hospital-based multidisciplinary
team designed to assess and respond to cases of suspected

neglect and abuse of elderly persons. An overview of the structure of the team is followed by descriptions of the assessment process as undertaken by the various disciplines represented in the team. A discussion of the problems and benefits of implementing teams such as this in other hospitals is presented in the conclusion.

The Elder Assessment Team

The Elder Assessment Team (EAT) at Boston's Beth Israel Hospital was organized in October 1981 in response to Massachusetts State Law, Chapter 479, which mandates the reporting of abuse of elders residing in long term care institutions. Chapter 479 was later complemented by Chapter 604, which requires reporting of abuse of community dwelling elders. Clinical and administrative staff of Beth Israel Hospital recommended the implementation of a multidisciplinary team to assess suspected cases of abuse or neglect and to make recommendations to hospital administration for further action. To avoid potential accusatory interpretations for cases being evaluated for *suspected* abuse or neglect, the name 'Elder Assessment Team' (EAT) was chosen to identify the group. The work of this team is described below.

The referral and assessment process

There are 12 members on the Elder Assessment Team: 5 nurses, 3 social workers, 3 physicians, and 1 health policy and ethics specialist. The team evaluates referred cases during the regular work week, with nursing coordinators initiating assessments on nights and weekends. The entire team meets weekly to review and discuss referred cases, as well as questions of policy, educational programming, and research activities.

Referrals

The assessment process is triggered by a referral, usually from a member of the hospital staff but occasionally from a community agency worker, the patient, or his family. The Elder Assessment Team has encouraged hospital staff to report to the team any suspicious injury or condition in an elder patient. It was believed that encouraging 'over reporting' to the EAT would decrease the likelihood of missing cases of abuse or neglect, would sensitize staff to the problem of elder abuse, and would provide teaching opportunities on this and other related geriatric issues.

Preliminary assessment
Initially, all referrals prompted a comprehensive evaluation
by a team nurse, physician, and social worker, and underwent
weekly team review. As the skill and confidence of the team
members have grown, a preliminary assessment is now conducted
by the team member receiving the initial referral. He or she
may decide that no further action is necessary. If suspicion
of neglect or abuse continues, primary responsibility for
coordinating the ongoing assessment is assigned to a team
nurse, physician, or social worker, depending on the nature
of the event or condition that triggered the referral.

Multidisciplinary assessment
The multidisciplinary assessment is conducted by team members
from nursing, medicine, and social work, each of whom com-
pletes a section of the assessment form (Fulmer et al., 1984).
Procedures include reviewing the patient's recent and past
medical records; interviewing the patient and family members,
if possible; examining the patient; and talking with the
direct care providers in the nursing home or community as
well as the direct care providers in the hospital. Information gathered includes level of care required, degree of
dependency, current and past mental and medical status, and
description of events leading to hospitalization.

Presentation of case to EAT
The case is then presented at the regular weekly meeting of
the EAT. Primary hospital care providers are invited to
participate in the case presentation and discussion. To
fulfill the legal mandate and to provide ongoing consultation, the team may decide: (1) to gather more information
before making a decision; (2) not to report the case because
the assessment does not support the suspicion of abuse or
neglect; or (3) to report the case to hospital administration for formal action.

Assessment outcomes
Primary care providers both within and outside the hospital
are provided with appropriate information regarding the
assessment and its outcome. Because the referred cases are
frequently difficult patients to care for due to multiple
health and functional problems, the team is often able to
make helpful suggestions for ongoing patient care. The
primary caretaker outside the hospital is notified by letter

about the outcome of the assessment. The team recognizes and commends evidence of good care whenever possible.

Should an administrative response be indicated, the hospital administration makes the formal report to the Department of Elder Affairs or the Department of Public Health. Under the state reporting law, however, any member of the hospital staff, including members of the assessment team, may make a formal report at any time.

Multidisciplinary participation

Each discipline represented on the team has specific skills and strategies in the assessment process.

Nursing assessment occurs at two levels. Primary nurses in the emergency, inpatient, or home care units screen patients and provide a majority of referrals to the EAT nurse. This level of nursing assessment includes baseline data regarding the patient's initial presentation and observations of the patient's clothing, hygiene, nutrition status, and skin integrity. A physical assessment notes bruising, contractures, dehydration, decubiti, or other abnormal or unusual signs. The patient's usual lifestyle, pattern of ambulation, elimination, feeding, ability to self-medicate, manage finances, and evidence of family involvement are documented, if possible. If this first level assessment results in a referral, an EAT nurse performs the second level assessment. Pertinent data are gathered by contacting other care providers familiar with the patient's history, (e.g., nursing home or visiting nurse personnel). Inquiry about the patient's condition prior to arrival at the hospital often adds an historical perspective that helps explain the patient's presentation. The EAT nurse also visits the patient, conducts a physical examination, and discusses the patient's view of caretaking and condition, if possible. The first and second level nursing assessments are recorded on the EAT form and are presented to the team for discussion with a recommendation for further action.

Social workers from inpatient or ambulatory service conduct an assessment of the patient and his or her social and psychological situation. This involves a two-part evaluation: (1) indepth interviews with patient, family, caretaker, and housestaff; and (2) a chart review. The patient's psychological, cultural, ethnic, religious, and economic background are considered, including relationships with care providers, social supports, financial management, interactions with family, friends, and ability to express needs. In particular, when families are involved, observa-

tions regarding patterns of communication and decision-making
are carefully noted. Perceptions of the problem are elicited
from family caretakers or nursing home staff, as appropriate.

Team physicians' roles include: (1) developing medical
criteria used for the characterization of referred patients;
(2) participating in evaluation and follow-up of individual
patients; (3) providing medical education relevant to elder
abuse and neglect; and (4) consulting on the medical approaches most likely to help in the patient's convalescence
and prevention of similar crises. This process includes review of the medical record, clarification of data within
that record from attending physicians and housestaff, and a
focused examination of the patient. The physicians bring to
the team knowledge of the medical system and provide a
necessary communication link to the physicians responsible
for the care of individual patients. In the physician's
assessment, particular attention is paid to documentation of
the nature and degree of injuries, the pattern of drug use
or administration, and the description of alterations in
mental status.

Ethical and policy issues are the focus of a social
scientist who facilitates consideration of difficult ethical
problems. The team frequently is faced with value conflicts
in balancing wishes to protect family units and individual
autonomy with the requirements of the reporting law and the
interests of the various individuals and institutions
involved in the case. Careful attention to team process and
relationships with other institutions and the community, as
well as issues of confidentiality, professional ethics, and
institutional practices has helped the team to weather the
difficult task of defining a new role in the institution and
to develop and maintain positive relationships with state
and community agencies.

Implementations of abuse assessment teams in other settings

Evaluation of the Beth Israel Hospital EAT by hospital
administration indicates that the team has been successful
in raising the awareness of elder abuse and neglect, in
educating staff to recognize signs and symptoms of potential
abuse and neglect, and in developing an effective process
for assessing suspected cases of abuse and neglect. The
implementation of similar assessment teams in other hospitals is certainly desirable and can be adapted to the
setting. Regular participation of multiple representatives
of four disciplines adds to the richness of the team but may

not be feasible or practical in settings with more limited resources. Health care providers who identify themselves as gerontological/geriatric specialists in a given setting should establish the elder abuse screening process. For some settings, a beeper or on-call system may be more practical than establishing a new resource group. When the on-call individual is asked to assess elder abuse, such state and local resources as departments of social service or elder affairs may be called upon to offer guidance. The support of the hospital administration is a key element to a successful program.

Impact of the elder assessment team

The EAT process places the burden of peer review on care providers designated to screen for elder abuse. Although the state requires that all cases of suspected abuse, neglect, and mistreatment are to be reported, the vague definition of 'suspected' lends itself to a variety of responses. The consequences of a report of abuse may include several negative and unintended outcomes, including disruption of family care provider systems, alienation of nursing homes, and retribution to the elder victim. Often, the care providers are devoted to the elderly person and are unaware that their actions may be detrimental to the elder's well-being. In fact, the multiplicity of the elder's health problems may create a situation in which the choice is made not to treat a specific symptom in order to sustain a functional capability may be reviewed as neglect.

Reports on elder abuse or neglect may have substantial impact on family members. If the suspected abuse occurred in a nursing home, the family may refuse to let their relative return, even if it is later determined that no abuse had occurred. The mere suspicion may cause alarm and the patient may then suffer the disruption of an unnecessary transfer. If it is the family member himself who is suspected of abusing the elder, he may resign from any obligation to the elder. Family members may also react with great indignation and consider such a report as libelous. Clearly, it is a sensitive process with many potential arenas for conflict.

These factors converge to place great importance on the validity of a formal report of suspected abuse. The individual care provider who is aware of these issues may be reluctant to report cases of suspected abuse unless the evidence is very clear. These considerations led to the formation of an on-site team to screen cases of suspected abuse to recommend whether a formal report should be made to the appropriate state agency. A review of the more than 50 cases referred to the EAT for assessment thus far and conversations with hospital staff indicate that staff are, indeed, aware of the potential for elder abuse and comfortable in referring cases to the EAT with relatively sketchy evidence of abuse or neglect. Their confidence that a multidisciplinary team will carefully investigate the cause for their suspicion provides comfort in reporting suspicions of elder abuse. Improved reporting of symptoms in practice will improve clinical understanding of elder abuse, which is a major aid in its prevention.

References

Block, M.R. and J.D. Sinnott. *The Battered Elder Syndrome: An Exploratory Study*, 1979. College Park, MD: Center on Aging, University of Maryland.

Douglass, R. 'The Michigan Abuse Study: Methodological Issue in Case Findings,' Nov. 1979. Paper presented at the 32nd Annual Meeting of the Gerontological Society, Washington, DC.

Fulmer, T., K. Carr and S. Street. 'Abuse of the Elderly: Screening and Detection,' *Journal of Emergency Nursing*, 1984, 10: 131-40

Lau, E.E. and J.I. Kosberg. 'Abuse of the Elderly by Informal Care Givers,' *Aging*, 1979, 299: 10-15

O'Malley, H.C., H.D. Segal and R. Perez. *Elder Abuse in Massachusetts: A Survey of Professionals and Paraprofessionals*, 1979. Boston: Legal Research and Services for the Elderly.

Walsh, B.K. 'Granny Bashing,' *Nursing Mirror*, 1977, 145: 32-34

Reprinted with permission from the Gerontological Society of America. The paper appeared in *The Gerontologist*, Vol. 26, April 1986, pp. 115-18.

1   Kathleen Carr, RN; Gretchen Dix, RN, MS; Terry Fulmer, RN, PhD; William Kavesh, MD; Liebe Kravitz, ACSW; Jane Matlaw, ACSW; Jane Mayer, ACSW; Kenneth Minaker, MD; Michael Shapiro, MD; Shirley Street, RN; Terrie Wetle, PhD; Nancy Zarle, RN. Contact: Terrie Wetle, PhD., Division of Health Policy Research and Education, 641 Huntington Avenue, Boston, MA 02115

6
THE PROTECTION OF ELDERLY MENTALLY INCOMPETENT INDIVIDUALS WHO ARE VICTIMS OF ABUSE
GILBERT SHARPE

Some elderly persons living in the community are at risk of serious harm resulting from abuse, but are lacking the capacity to take steps to extricate themselves from the abusive situation. The abuse may take on the form of deliberate harm, sexual abuse, neglect or abandonment. These victims of abuse are often terrorized and unable to report the abuse.

Although the abuse may involve acts of physical violence or severe neglect of a potentially criminal nature, the criminal justice system usually cannot provide protection to the abused adult.

There is no legislation authorizing access to the abused person and enabling social services and health officials to intervene to protect the person.

In recent years, our law has come a long way to protect the rights of the elderly in a number of areas. For example, the *Powers of Attorney Act*, which first appeared in 1979, enables someone to execute a power of attorney appointing anyone to act on behalf of their assets, such power to continue even should the person become mentally incompetent to look after their assets. Recent amendments to that statute and to the Mental Health Act extend this power to, for example, a person suffering from Alzheimer's disease, to so appoint an individual with a power of attorney that even survives admission to a psychiatric facility where the Public Trustee would usually take control of the assets.

Also, as we know there is a current debate surrounding mandatory retirement, with much support for the position that human rights legislation preventing discrimination on account of age that makes an exception for matters such as mandatory retirement itself infringes the *Charter of Rights*. In fact, currently all three political parties at the federal level are working on policy papers that might eventually result in the removal of mandatory retirement ages entirely.

However, little has been done to address the significant problem of what has euphemistically been described as 'granny bashing.'

Case example
In the following assault case, documented by the Scarborough Health Department, there was a critical delay as a result of the lack of clear authority to intervene.

A 60 year old woman suffering from Alzeheimer's disease was showing evidence of bruising, malnutrition, and lack of physical and medical care. She lived with her daughter's common-law husband who had a criminal record for assault. She appeared to be terrified, and was unable to describe what had happened to her. Without her evidence as a basis for laying charges, it appeared that no legal action was possible.

The situation was referred to the police by the public health nurse involved in the case. After lengthy delay and hesitation because of the lack of clear legal authority to enter the home and investigate, the police finally forced entry. The woman was found hidden in a closet and badly beaten.

Limitations of using the criminal justice system

In suspected abuse or neglect cases, the option of prosecuting the offender should always be considered. Under the Criminal Code, the following are some of the charges that might be laid: assault (s.245), assault causing bodily harm (s.245.1), sexual assault (s.246.1), aggravated sexual assault (s.246.3), sexual offences of certain types including incest (s.150), and sexual intercourse with a female ward, step-daughter or foster daughter (s.153), failure to provide necessaries of life to a person under one's charge who is unable to withdraw from that charge and to provide himself with the necessaries of life (s.197), and failure to complete an act which has been undertaken, where the omission is potentially dangerous to life (s.199). Section 197 provides that everyone is under a legal duty to provide necessaries of life to a person under his charge if that person is unable by reason of age to withdraw himself from that charge and is unable to provide himself with necessaries of life.

Where physical abuse is suspected, the police have
authority to investigate. Any information of assault may be
laid independent of a complaint or evidence of the victim,
provided that there is other evidence of assault (such as
the presence of bruising or lacerations). However, for
prosecution to proceed, there must be enough to charge a
specific person with an offence. In cases where an elderly
person is being abused, there may be evidence of a crime but
it may not be possible to ascertain and prove beyond a
reasonable doubt the identity of the perpetrator. In short,
while the abused person may be at serious risk, there may
not be a legally provable case of assault that could be
dealt with under the Criminal Code.

Moreover, prosecution of criminal offences, while important, has its focus on the offender. Protection for the
victim and assistance in finding a solution to the burden of
living in an abusive situation are often left unresolved.

Provincial legislation: access and protection

At present, Ontario has no legislation that would authorize
intervention appropriate to these circumstances. Access to
the abusive situation is of primary importance in protecting
victims and preventing further abuse. While powers of access
are available under numerous statutes, none has as its purpose the provision of protection and assistance to an en-
dangered or abused mentally incapable adult.

Existing protective legislation does not authorize
intervention or contain a statutory duty to intervene to
protect mentally incapable victims of abuse. The *Mental
Health Act* authorizes protective intervention where an
individual suffering from a mental disorder is a danger to
him or herself or to others, and requires that individual to
be taken to a psychiatric facility. It is not a vehicle for
providing protection to a victim of abuse. Indeed, the
Mental Health Act is not and should never be viewed as a
panacea for all of society's ills, as it once was years ago
when the back wards of our mental hospitals were filled with
all sorts of disadvantaged individuals. No civil committal
statute has as a criterion for committal the lack of mental
capacity of the person. Mental illness does not necessarily
mean mental incompetency. Thus, to intrude into someone's
life in circumstances where that person is not a threat
to themselves or others as a result of mental illness, extra

protections must exist. One of these would require apparent
mental incapacity, and another, the involvement of the judi-
cial system. While this may leave unprotected a few persons
who are not a threat as a result of a mental illness, who
have capacity, but who cannot extricate themselves from an
abusive situation, societal interference here will have to
be premised on the commission of a criminal act.

The *Health Protection and Promotion Act* does not contain
any provision that sould allow for intervention on behalf of
an abused adult.

The *Mental Incompetency Act* provides for guardianship of
the person and the estate of a mentally incompetent adult.
The statute does not in any way address the immediate
issue of abuse of a mentally incapable individual. Furthermore, an individual who is suffering from abuse and who
lacks the capacity to extricate him or herself from the
situation is not necessarily in need of a guardian. Once the
cycle of abuse has been broken, the victim may become quite
capable of functional decision-making on their own.

Current practice
Currently, in practice, social service and health personnel
utilize voluntary measures to their limit. Collaborative
effort among police, health and social service professionals
have resulted in effective assistance to the abused person
in some cases. Occasionally, field workers have gained
access to the premises under the authority of the *Ontario
Society for the Prevention of Cruelty to Animals Act* where
an animal as well as a human being was in distress. Where a
person subject to abuse is receiving family benefits, the
worker may gain access to the home for the purpose of a
home visit and, in doing so, find evidence of the abuse.
Sometimes field workers have felt it imperative to intervene
without authority to protect an abused adult and have done
so in spite of the legal risk to themselves. In other
instances, however, situations of apparent abuse have
continued because there has been no legal means of intervention.

A clear need has been identified for legislative authority to protect mentally incapable adults who are the victims
of abuse. Existing mechanisms are inadequate to ensure a
prompt, effective response when it becomes apparent that a
mentally disabled individual residing in the community is at
risk of serious abuse.

Proposed model for intervention to protect mentally
incapable victims of abuse

a) Basic principles

This proposal for intervention to protect mentally
incapable individuals in the community who are the victims
of abuse is based on the following principles:

Mentally incapable persons are entitled to society's
protection.

In intervening to assist a mentally incapable person who
is a victim of abuse, the least restrictive alternative
should be employed to protect the individual *without
unduly* infringing on their privacy and personal freedom.

To the greatest extent consistent with providing the
needed protection, the procedural rights of the abused
adult must be preserved.

To the greatest extent consistent with providing the
needed protection, the integrity and autonomy of the
family unit should be respected.

It must be emphasized that any proposed model for intervention is premised on the assumption that voluntary
measures have been tried and have failed. Primary emphasis
must always be on the provision of support services in the
community. However, a point is sometimes reached where,
regardless of the community resources available, access to a
suspected abusive situation is blocked. How much money is
sufficient when the door to the home will not be opened?
Clearly, much of this discussion involves balancing need and
right. The rights of both the victim and their family to be
let alone and the need to help the victim where they are
unable to assist themselves. It is for this reason that the
criteria and parameters for intervention must be made as
clear and objective as possible.

b) Criteria for determining need for intervention to protect
   victims of abuse

There is a need for authority to intervene to protect
those elderly persons living in the community who are at
risk of harm resulting from abuse. Mentally disabled indi-

viduals who are unable to take steps to leave an abusive
situation or to provide evidence regarding assaults they
have suffered are particularly vulnerable to abuse perpetrated by their custodians.

Abuse of the mentally disabled may be chronic, resulting
in serious harm being inflicted over a prolonged period of
time, or may develop into an emergency situation where
crisis treatment is required. Where cases of repeated assault and extreme neglect have come to the attention of
health units, efforts to provide protection to the abused
adult are thwarted by the lack of legal authority to intervene. While this proposal would not in any way derogate
from the onus to prosecute the offender in a case of
abuse, it recognizes that criminal prosecution may not
provide the immediate protection and support needed by the
abused adult. There is a clear need for a mechanism to
provide protective services that meet the immediate need of
the victim of abuse.

Under this proposal, involuntary protective services
could be provided to an abuse victim where *all* of the
following criteria are met.

1) There are reasonable and probable grounds to believe that
   an individual is being abused.

Abuse, in this context would be defined as follows: a
condition of i) actual serious harm or substantial risk
of serious harm resulting from deliberate action or failure
of custodian to protect; ii) sexual abuse; iii) the non-
provision of necessaries of life or medical treatment,
resulting in risk of serious harm; iv) abandonment.

An important issue involves whether the definition should
focus only on physical harm. Non-physical (emotional) abuse
crestes problems because of the difficulty of reliably
determining the presence of emotional harm as demonstrated
by difficulties encountered under the *Child Welfare Act* with
reporting emotional abuse.

2) There are reasonable and probable grounds to believe
   that the abused individual lacks the mental capacity to
   take steps to extricate him or herself from the abusive
   situation.

This proposal for protective services is directed to
individuals in an abusive situation who are unable to formulate a request to leave or to take the necessary steps to

remove him or herself from the situation. Such individuals would not, on their own initiative, be able to rely on the criminal justice system to alleviate the situation.

3) Reasonable efforts have been made, and documented, to gain voluntary access to the individual to provide protection and appropriate services, with the result that access has not been granted and the services have not been accepted on a voluntary basis.

Access to the abused individual is critical to the provision of appropriate protective services and prevention of further abuse. However, before involuntary action is pursued, reasonable efforts to gain access to the individual and provide services on a voluntary basis would be required. The involvement of a Medical Officer of Health (or his/her delegate) would be required to investigate the situation of alleged abuse and attempt voluntary intervention before seeking an order to intervene involuntarily.

4) The provisions would be directed to adults aged 18 years and over, and children 16 to 18 years who are not in the care of Children's Aid Society and who have no legal guardian.

This criterion is designed to ensure that prospective intervention is available for mentally incapable adults and those children who fall outside the purview of the child welfare legislation.

c) Key features of the intervention

The major components of the intervention would be:

Access to the individual
Where there are reasonable and probable grounds to suspect that a mentally incapable adult is being abused, and attempts to investigate the situation and provide support services on a voluntary basis are being resisted, a legally enforceable right to access to the allegedly abused person is essential.
Medical Officers of Health, through evidence gathered by their staff, would be responsible for determining whether or not there were reasonable and probable grounds to suspect abuse.

The primary intent of the access provision would be to assess accurately the situation and examine the abused person in order to determine what protective services are needed.

Taking the individual to a place of safety
Once a case of suspected abuse has been assessed, the best course of action may be to closely monitor the situation and provide support services in the home environment. For some mentally handicapped adults, removal from even an abusive home may be extremely traumatic. The wishes and best interests of the subject would be determinants of the nature of the protective services to be extended.

However, in some cases it will be essential to remove the abused person to a place of safety for their protection. Voluntary removal of the person from the living situation may be accomplished by agreement. The authority to remove the person involuntarily where there is no such agreement would be an essential component of the proposed legislation.

Depending on the abused person's medical condition, an appropriate place of safety might be a public hospital or a nursing home.

Admitting and keeping the person in a place of safety
The proposal would include the corresponding authority to admit and keep the person in a place of safety. In the case of an abused person, a protective custody order would be time-limited, with the emphasis on treatment of injury and removal of the risk or cause of abuse in the home. Such an order would be extendable, based on medically-supported need for further treatment and evidence of risk of remaining in the home situation.

d) The process

Granting authority to intervene
When a situation of alleged abuse of a mentally incapable adult is discovered, action may be required on an urgent basis.

A two-option process is proposed for authorizing the intervention, either of which could be employed to deal with a situation of suspected abuse.

1. A statutory power would be granted to Medical Officers of Health to intervene at their discretion. The statutory

power would extend to entering the premises where the
alleged abuse was occurring, observing and examining the
abused person, assessing the situation and providing
emergency treatment if required. If the Medical Officer
of Health determined that the abused person should be
taken to a place of safety, they would be required to
apply to a Justice of the Peace or court for a protective
service order.

2. The second option would be a procedure that could be
   initiated by anyone to obtain a protective service order
   in the form of a warrant authorizing a specified person
   to enter the premises where the alleged abuse was taking
   place and to observe and examine the person and assess
   the situation. Depending on the evidence available, the
   order may also authorize emergency treatment if required
   and/or removal of the person to a place of safety.

As a variant on this second option, authority to make an
application to the Justice of the Peace or court could be
limited to the Medical Officer of Health, based on information obtained from any source.

Prerequisites to ordering intervention
Prior to intervention being undertaken, either with or without a warrant, the criteria that I described earlier for
determining when there is a need for involuntary intervention would have to be met.
The focus of the intervention would be on protecting and
assisting the victim.

Where a warrant was being sought, the court would not be
required to make a finding as to how the injury was inflicted or the identity of the perpetrator, as a condition for intervention.

The court may recommend that criminal proceedings be
launched against a likely perpetrator, but a protection
order would not be dependent on a finding of guilt in
such proceedings.

Similarily, a decision by a Medical Officer of Health to
exercise the proposed statutory authority to gain access to
assess the situation of an allegedly abused adult should be

taken independently of considerations of the possibility or likelihood of criminal proceedings against the offender(s).

The order
Two types of protective service orders are proposed, depending on what would best serve the needs and interests of the abused adult:

i) A protective supervision order:

would authorize specific person(s) to have access to the living situation and the abused person for the purpose of protecting that person;

would be of short duration;

would contain an automatic termination date but would be renewable by the Justice of the Peace or court upon presentation of evidence of need for renewal.

In making an order, the court would be empowered to attach reasonable conditions to assist in the provision of services.

ii) A temporary protective care and custody order:

would authorize removal of the victim from their living situation and admittance to a place of safety;

would authorize treatment of injuries caused by abuse, where the victim is unable to consent to treatment;

would be time-limited and subject to review;

would be renewable based on evidence of need for further treatment and/or continued presence of risk in the home situation.

Where the victim of abuse was capable of consenting to care and treatment, their consent would be obtained prior to proceeding.
A protective service order of either proposed type would be carried out by a Medical Officer of Health assisted, where appropriate, by their staff, or by a police officer.

e) Mandatory reporting requirement

One might consider the principle of mandatory reporting provision, requiring persons who have reasonable grounds to suspect that a mentally incapable adult is being subjected to abuse to report those suspicions to a designated authority. This would be analogous to the reporting requirements under the Child Welfare Act. The *Neglected Adults Welfare Act* in Newfoundland is the only Canadian precedent of which I am aware. Does one then establish an 'Adult Aid Society?' Many feel that this would take the principle of 'parens patriae' too far. However, it is a concept worth examining.

f) Follow-up

An adult who is being abused, and who lacks the mental capacity to extricate him or herself from the abusive situation may be capable of functional decision-making in a supportive non-abusive environment. Once the cycle of abuse has been broken, there may be no further need for involuntary intervention.

However, if the person's mental incapacity were ongoing and they appeared to be in need of a guardian, an application for personal guardianship would be made on their behalf. The proposed legislation would include provisions for temporary guardianship, where needed, to fill the gap between crisis intervention and the appointment of a guardian of the person.

Conclusion

There is a need for new legislative provisions to authorize access to and protection from abuse for mentally incapable adults at risk in the community. The required new legislation could be separate from or integrated with new legislation for personal guardianship.

This paper appeared in Mayor Mel Lastman's Task Force on Abuse of the Elderly Proceedings, October 1985, pp. 21-36. Reproduced with permission of the author and the office of Mayor Lastman.

7
ELDER ABUSE: SUMMARY OF RESULTS - MANITOBA
DONNA J. SHELL

Shell (1982) completed the first Canadian study related
to elder abuse. Interviews (N=105) were conducted within
all regions of the province - Winnipeg, Central, Norman,
Interlake, Parklands, Westman, and Eastman - thereby
representing both urban and rural areas and populations
ethnically and socioeconomically diverse. Respondent types
included public health nurses, social workers, psychiatric
nurses, Victorian Order of Nurses, RN's in home care programs as well as hospital settings, police officers, doctors,
lawyers, and clergy members. Risk reduction strategies are
presented and selected tables are being presented to summarize the findings of the study.

Risk reduction strategies

Central registry
One approach to risk reduction is the establishment and
maintenance of a central registry of all reported
information in cases of abuse. Mandatory reporting of abuse
cases to a central registry could provide immunity from
liability for anyone reporting a case in good faith. The
reports should be followed by immediate investigation of
cases. A registry would be useful in creating an awareness
of the extent of the problem as well as for identifying any
previous incidents of abuse recorded with respect to the
same individual and alerting protective services programs
so that an appropriate course of action can be taken. As
well as providing protection against continuing abuse, a
registry would, through the recording of types and
incidences of abuse, provide the data necessary for
research, program planning, and service improvement.

Seven Oaks has recognized the need for a registry of elder abuse and has implemented the first of its kind in Manitoba. Suspected cases of abuse encountered at the hospital are now being documented. Each report includes date, name, address, sex, and age, as well as information concerning the suspected type of abuse or potential risk situation (for example, a disabled elderly person living alone or with an infirm care provider). The name of the staff member reporting the suspected case is also recorded along with descriptions of any action taken. While the formation of a registry is a beginning and an important step in the direction of protection, it is of course not the total answer to the problem of abuse. It is merely a tool for the identification of abused elderly persons. In order adequately to handle cases of elder abuse the creation of avenues for protection and prevention is necessary and a full commitment to protection of elderly persons requires provision of a wide range of services and may call for large-scale action in legislation in order to provide effective programming.

Education
Education as a preventive measure would disseminate knowledge concerning aging and the needs and care requirements of the aged. Many caregivers may require information concerning practical problems such as budgeting, meal planning and nutrition. Additionally, informal group discussions could be useful methods of counselling families caring for elderly members, especially those identified as being at risk, to become more patient and more understanding of the importance of sound information concerning elder care and the importance of their roles. Caregiver education and counselling could help the caregiver gain relief from feelings of frustration or anger brought on by the responsibility of caring for a dependent adult, and subsequently to deal with their feelings other than through physical force or other forms of mistreatment.

Education of caregivers in high risk situations could be carried out by carefully selected and well-trained volunteers who would serve as adjuncts to a social agency's professional staff. Also, volunteers, as well as providing information and referral services, could visit with families and help caregivers with day-to-day problems. The development of programs to recruit and train volunteers could be beneficial to all in that the numbers of abusive and high

risk situations that could be reached would be expanded.
Such programs would also allow professionals a greater
amount of time for group and individual counselling.

Crisis intervention
The crisis intervention model is based on the premise that
'any hazardous event upsets the emotional balance of individuals and families and creates serious problems of readjustment' (Thorman 1981:56). Studies of abusing families
suggest that in many cases a crisis in the family's life
situation has precipitated abuse. A caregiver's ability to
cope with crisis depends not only on inner resources but
also on the community resources available to help resolve
the situation and aid in readjustment. Referral of caregivers
and older dependent adults facing difficult situations to
these resources could be crucial to the prevention of abuse.
    The training of law enforcement officers in early and
effective intervention techniques involving referral to
helping agencies has proven to be beneficial. An interesting
example is provided by a family intervention training ex-
periment undertaken in West Harlem. A month-long training
program was provided to officers, and included lectures,
workshops, field trips, and role playing (Thorman 1981:157).
To determine the effectiveness of the training a comparison
of the experimental unit was made with a regular precinct
unit. It was found that the precinct unit made no referrals
to social and mental health agencies, while the experimental
unit made referrals to twenty such agencies in 55 per cent
of all cases of family violence encountered.

Advocacy
The risk reduction strategies discussed above call for the
establishment of a wide range of social services that reach
out to elderly persons at risk. These services could include
homemaker and housekeeping services, day care facilities,
financial aid for families caring for an older dependent
adult, and workers to escort clients through the various
agencies. Since the abused elderly can often not protect or
speak for themselves, advocacy programs and services must
also be developed. 'Advocacy' is defined as the 'ability
to fight for the rights and dignity of people in need of
help ... fighting for services on behalf of a single client
or segments of society.' (Thorman 1981:69). It has been
suggested that advocate programs emanate from an organiza-
tional base employing volunteers backed by professional

staff (Cohen 1978:38). These volunteers would play the role of 'agents' and could, for example, develop fiduciary relationships with those older persons requiring assistance. This would involve the consent of the elderly individual that the agent act on his/her behalf. The agent would be under obligations similar to those imposed upon a trustee, i.e. 'to act with the utmost good faith ... for the furtherance and advancement of the interests of one's principal' (Cohen 1978:38). Cohen further suggests that agents be volunteers rather than social workers since the ability of a social worker to act as an agent would be severely limited by the sheer size of the caseload with which the worker must already contend.

Advocates for the elderly could work for legislative reforms, public enlightenment and assistance, and the creation of new services such as shelters, legal, medical, housing, and counselling services, and the linkage of clients to the system of services that meet their needs. The public is largely uninformed about the extent and nature of elder abuse. A lack of awareness, and probably denial, accounts for some of the silence that has surrounded the issue. According to the *Star* (1980:346), the lack of adequate services for victims and abusers corresponds, in part, to the lack of knowledge about the incidence of abuse. And since the establishment of a system of services needs a wide base of support, advocacy programs could also provide public information through media coverage in order to promote an awareness of problems, and for example, the distribution of brochures which would help educate and sensitize the public to the nature of the problem as well as increase professional awareness. The education of professionals in the area of elder abuse (and their involvement in program planning) is essential to program support and to working for new legislation and policies. It is an emotionally charged subject, but only through public and professional awareness of the existence of the problem can help be offered to both victims and abusers.

Through advocacy programs the elderly would be more likely to receive the assistance required to help solve the problems confronting them. Such programs would also advocate for the caregivers. In both cases, this could range from, for example, those who have sought, and been denied, financial assistance and those who would benefit by being accompanied through the legal procedures involved in applications for assistance, to enlisting the assistance of a legal aid representative to advocate for a person in regard to eviction.

Advocacy programs could take a multi-disciplinary approach similar to child protection programs. Members of various professions would participate so that the base of knowledge and experience for the making of decisions and recommendations would be expanded. Primary team members might include social workers to assume the responsibility for evaluating the safety of the home and treatment strategies; physicians and psychiatrists to act as diagnostic experts in cases of abuse; coordinators to coordinate the efforts of the different agencies involved; attorneys for clarification of legal matters; law enforcement officers, since they may become directly involved initially; and public health nurses to assume responsibility for delivery of health care services. This multi-disciplinary team would periodically review cases to determine plans of action, and to revise plans in light of new information and new needs, and formulate preliminary and long-term recommendations.

Summary of findings in tabular form

This study finds financial abuse to be the most frequently encountered type of abuse of elderly persons, followed by psychosocial and physical. The data suggest that of all reported instances of abuse, the greatest percentage of financial and psychosocial abuse cases were encountered by public health nurses while social workers encountered the greatest percentage of physical abuse cases.

Tables 1, 2, and 3 present the dimensions in each category of abuse and the relative frequency with which they were encountered.

TABLE 1
Per cent of instances of financial abuse by dimensions of
financial abuse

Dimension	Per cent
Cashing pension/social insurance cheques and with-holding the means for daily living necessities	50.4
Trickery, fraud, misappropriated/misused property	10.3
Theft of funds and/or possessions	9.8
Trickery, fraud, misappropriated/misused funds	8.9
Grossly overcharged for residence	6.7
Taking pension/social insurance cheque or other funds through threats or force	5.8
Grossly overcharged for small services and/or items	3.1

TABLE 2
Per cent of instances of psychosocial abuse by dimensions
of psychosocial abuse

Dimension	Per cent
Verbal/emotional: derogation, humiliation, intimdation, infantilization, or any treatment diminishing identity, dignity, or self-worth	38.6
Inadequate attention in terms of time, concern, and understanding of needs; left unattended for extended periods of time	17.5
Isolation	13.9
Confinement	11.2
Removal from active participation in one's own life	7.2
Threats of harm or violence	6.8
Threats of withholding assistance, abandonment, or institutionalization	4.8

TABLE 3
Per cent of instances of physical abuse by dimensions of
physical abuse

Dimension	Per cent
Physical assault	35.1
Withholding food	11.7
Rough handling, pushing, or shoving resulting in injuries or discomfort	11.0

Dimension	Per cent
Gross neglect resulting from avoidance of needs for assistance with daily living (eg. personal and hygienic care)	11.0
Withholding medication and/or medical attention	7.8
Injuries resulting from avoidance of needs for assistance	5.2
Deliberate over-medication (pills or alcohol)	5.2
Sexual assault	4.5
Homicide	3.9
Physically restrained (tied, gagged)	2.6
Injuries resulting from deliberate hazardous situations	1.9

The abused elders and the abusers

This study finds 67.7 per cent of identified abused elderly persons to be female while 32.2 per cent are male. The data further suggest that the most frequently abused elderly person is a female aged 80-84 years, residing with a family member for 10 or more years. (Table 4)

TABLE 4
Per cent of abused elders by living arrangement and by length of residence with caregiver

Living arrangement	Per cent	Length of residence with caregiver	Per cent
Live alone	30.1	4 or fewer years	26.3
Reside with caregiver	69.9	5-9 years	17.4
		10+ years	56.2

N = 402

Abuser characteristics are presented in Tables 5 and 6. As the data in Table 5 suggest, 24.4 per cent of all abusers of elderly persons identified in this study are unrelated caregivers while 75.6 per cent are family members of which 60 per cent are males. As indicated, the son is the most frequent abuser followed closely by the daughter.

Of all abusive caregivers identified in this study, 36.3 per cent were found to be over 60 years of age. Table 6 presents the age distribution of caregivers over the age of 60.

TABLE 5
Per cent of abusing caregivers within each category of relationship to victim

Relationship	Per cent
Son*	23.6
Daughter*	21.2
Husband	16.4
Wife	4.5
Brother	3.7
Sister	2.2
Niece	1.7
Nephew	1.2
Grandchildren	1.0
Unrelated caregiver	24.4

N=402
*Includes in-laws

Table 6
Per cent of caregivers by age cohort 60 years of age and over

Age	Per cent
60-69	48.0
70-79	31.5
80+	20.5
	100.0

N = 146 (36.3%)

High risk factors related to abuse

Respondents were asked to identify factors which, in their opinion and experience, were indicators of situations with a high risk of potential abuse for elderly persons. Tables 7 and 8 present these high risk indicators concerning elderly persons and caregivers respectively.

Table 7
Per cent of respondents identifying high risk factors
concerning elderly persons

Factor	Per cent
Physical impairment	24.8
Suspicious physical injuries	24.8
Mental status (eg. confused, unstable)	22.9
Depression, withdrawal, anger	18.1
Lack of family supports	13.3
Poor family relationship	13.3
Overcrowding	10.5
Social isolation	7.6
Wealth or many assets	7.6
Residing with family member	7.6
Extremely demanding and difficult	6.7
Geographic isolation	4.8
Living alone	4.8
Other	11.4

N=105

Table 8
Per cent of respondents identifying high risk factors
concerning caregivers

Factor	Per cent
Alcoholism	44.8
Financial stress	15.2
Poor attitude toward aging	10.5
Poor coping ability and emotional resources	8.6
Age 60 and over	5.7
Mentally unstable	5.7

N=105

Mandatory reporting

Respondents' opinions regarding the issues of mandatory
reporting of elder abuse cases to a central registry, the
formation of a protocol and legislation specifically
concerning elder abuse, and the formation of advisory
committees are presented in Table 9.

Table 9
Per cent of opinions regarding mandatory reporting,
protocol, legislation, and advisory committee

Favourability towards:	Yes	Under certain conditions only	No	Undecided
Mandatory reporting	81.0	7.6	6.7	4.8
Protocol	87.6	1.9	5.7	4.8
Legislation	84.8	1.9	8.6	4.8
Advisory committee	88.6	3.8	6.7	1.0

N=105

As indicated in Table 9, the majority of respondents were
in favour of mandatory reporting to a central registry, the
formation of a protocol, legislation, and advisory committees.
The 7.6 per cent of responses indicating favourability towards mandatory reporting of abuse cases under certain conditions only, included conditions in which the reported information would contain no names and be used strictly for
research purposes, and the condition that mandatory reporting
apply only to life-threatening or unresolvable situations.
Also included under favourability towards mandatory reporting
under certain conditions only, were stipulations that financial and psychosocial abuse not be included, the rationale
being that these areas are best resolved through counselling
rather than law, and that psychosocial abuse in particular
is too subtle and determinations too subjective to be identifiable with any degree of certainty.

Conclusions

The findings reported here, while representing only a first
step toward exploring the extent and nature of elder abuse,
raise some interesting questions and suggest further areas
for future research and issues for program development. The
development of interview items designed to tap further areas
of the problem, areas not explored in the present study,
might include questions concerning the relationship between
elder abuse and disability related dependency. More detailed
and elaborate research in the area of elder abuse would be
helpful for developing criteria for case identification,
direction for planning intervention and prevention strategies, and providing a foundation for change in social policy

or legislation. Thus, a major objective of future research should be the identification of effective means for isolating elder abuse cases. Hence, primary contributing factors or conditions in situations of abuse must be described with sufficient confidence to give professionals some guidelines in identifying potential cases. So also, the end product should be the identification of effective means for treating elder abuse and alleviating those conditions which appear to promote it.

References

Shell, D.J. *Protection of the Elderly: A Study of Elder Abuse, 1982*. Winnipeg, Manitoba. Manitoba Council on Aging, 1982

8
THE ELDERLY: ABUSE OR ABUSERS?
STANLEY E. GOLDSTEIN AND ARTHUR BLANK

There has been a sudden interest in the problem of abuse of
the elderly. Kimsey and associates[1] have stated that 'its
magnitude is probably substantial' and that it 'has been
overlooked, concealed and ignored'. Such a conclusion may be
oversimplistic. What is overlooked are the many factors
involved in the care of the elderly.

The elderly and society

Society's obligations towards the elderly must be met. Although we are a youth-oriented society, we are beginning to
provide geriatric day-care centres and outpatient hospital
programs, and we are turning away from statutory retirement
and towards the prohibition of discrimination by age. In
addition, training programs in geriatrics and psychogeriatrics continue to develop.
    In general, however, society tends to neglect the elderly.
In their own homes, institutions and homes of their relatives
the elderly feel unimportant, as if they have no real purpose
in life. Such is the real tragedy of old age. Although we try
in many ways to help care for and support the elderly, we
have yet to define a role for them that is acceptable to them
and those around them. The elderly and their caregivers or
families are caught together in emotional turmoils that they
often cannot comprehend and for which solutions are elusive.

The elderly and their children

The Bible says 'Honour thy father and thy mother' - there
is no mention of love in this context. Personality traits
that can be tolerated as long as the person is independent

become intolerable in the aged; for example, a person with a
'paranoid personality' may function well until he or she is
forced on others. Persons used to having their own way cannot tolerate the increasing dependence of aging. A wife who
has been taught to be dependent finds her needs ungratified
after her husband dies.

Most children of the elderly do their best to help. They
do not 'dump' or 'force' the parent into an institution;
rather, guilt may keep them trying when common sense tells
them to quit. When the caregivers - children, spouses or
institutions - cannot cope they are criticized by friends,
relatives, society, and often the medical profession. It is
easy to sympathize and identify with the sick or helpless
elderly person.

Steinmetz[2] has noted that 'parenting a parent can frus-
trate the middle-aged child's financial and emotional goals'.
The children of the elderly are sandwiched between the demands of their parents and of their own children. With the
limited emotional resources of the children it is not sur-
prising that a helpless and confused parent can engender
rage. The passivity with which the elderly often express
anger is likewise capable of provoking aggression. However,
these impulses are rarely unleashed in spite of the tempta-
tion.

It is not uncommon for the elderly to complain about
neglect or abuse. Their losses are often irreplaceable, and
frustration and anger result. These feelings are usually
kept to themselves, leading to depressions, but may also be
projected onto others. They often ask for and need more help
and support than anyone can reasonably expect to receive.
For example, a parent whose spouse has died often moves to
be close to his or her child. The parent's expectations may
far exceed the child's capacity to give, the child having
his or her own life to live. The parent becomes bitter about
the 'neglect' and 'ingratitude', and the passive-aggressive
behaviour so common in the elderly intensifies the conflict.
This situation becomes intolerable for the child caught in
the midst of this rage and guilt.

The increasing numbers of 'confused' elderly persons
present a special problem to their caregivers. Lezak[3] has
correctly stated that 'one who has not cared for an ill,
helpless, confused old person may not comprehend the helplessness, rage and frustration involved.' Society does not
give a great deal of help to the caregivers who are left

drained, depressed and in despair. Moreover, the elderly
persons who are organically impaired tend to have less
control over impulses, deal poorly with frustration and are
emotionally labile. It is not uncommon for them to be
verbally and physically aggressive toward their caregivers,
and to some extent such action is accepted as part of the
illness. The caregivers rarely retaliate; they are more
likely to become overprotective.

The elderly and institutions

Institutions for the elderly have a difficult task and are
often used as scapegoats by relatives and patients. Although
some patients may not complain because they fear the withdrawal of the staff's goodwill, complaints from patients
are frequent. It is difficult to validate allegations of
abuse, especially when made by confused patients,[4] but
institutions are justifiably afraid of being accused of
abuse by relatives, politicians and lay people. They cannot
set reasonable limits and have no recourse when accusations
do arise. Thus, these caregivers are abused and unable to
counterattack. In no other setting would such aggression be
accepted.
    The inability of the staff to set limits of appropriate
behaviour often contributes to behaviour regression in the
patients. We criticize the caregivers for this but fail to
support them if they attempt to be firm. They are seen and
see themselves as being cruel. A detached observer will
agree with Shakespeare's dictum 'I must be cruel only to be
kind.' Shakespeare also noted that 'an old man is twice a
child.' We can deal with a child as a child; how do we deal
with the 'old man?'
    Nursing homes and other institutions for the elderly are
often faced with a damned-if-you-do and damned-if-you-don't
situation. They must tolerate the intolerable - the noisy,
violent or abusive patient. If the staff use sedatives to
control behaviour they are accused of turning the patients
into 'vegetables.' However, although it is reasonable that
the families of such patients will not take them home, they
often have little sympathy for the staff and unreasonably
expect them to manage somehow. In addition, the staff are
responsible if a patient runs away or falls. However, tying
a patient into a chair is seen by many as abuse.

The elderly and their money

That the elderly are easy targets for con artists is
familiar to everyone who reads a newspaper. However, they
are also susceptible to such manipulation by their 'loved
ones.' In Ontario, patients who have been declared incompetent can, depending on the circumstances, have their
assets protected by a public trustee. This can create
hardship for the spouse, who is denied access to such
assets. If a member of the family assumes the role of
caregiver, should he or she not use the patient's money? If
the patient's money is used, who decides when this privilege
is being abused? The answers to these problems are not
clear-cut. However, most elderly persons have the right to
do with their assets as they wish.

Summary

It cannot be disputed that the elderly are often physically,
verbally, psychologically and financially abused. However,
the problem can be overemphasized and viewed from only one
side. Most caregivers really do care; the most they can
probably be accused of is benign neglect or 'killing with
kindness.' However, although the attitudes of society are
changing, the elderly are still not seen as 'important;'
their feelings of self-worth are undermined and their roles
ill-defined.
   The relation between the elderly and their families is
complex. Although the lives of the aged are often difficult,
the problems of caregivers also deserve consideration. To
see the situation in terms of 'good and bad guys' is to miss
its essence. We can only help the elderly and the people
involved in their care if we see the difficulties from all
points of view.

References

1. Kimsey, L.R., A.R. Tarbox, and D.B. Bragg. 'Abuse of the
   Elderly - The Hidden Agenda. I. The caretakers and the
   categories of abuse,' *Journal of the American Geriatric
   Society*, 1981: 29: 465-472
2. Steinmetz, A. 'Battered Parent,' *Society*, 1978: 15: 54

3. Lezak, M.D. 'Living with the Characterologically Altered Brain Injured Patient, *Journal of Clinical Psychiatry*, 1978: 39: 592–8
4. Eisdorfer, C. 'Intellectual and congnitive changes in the aged.' In Busee, E.W. and E. Pfeiffer, eds. *Behaviour and Adaptation in Late Life*, 1969. Boston, MA: Little, Brown

Originally published in the *Canadian Medical Association Journal*, Vol. 127, 15 September 1982 and reprinted with permission of the Canadian Medical Association, and the authors.

9
FAMILY ABUSE OF THE ELDERLY
MISH VADASZ

Will the evidence of family violence ever end? Following the
issues of child abuse, spouse abuse and sexual abuse which
have been addressed in sequence over the past 20 years, we
must now face the painful facts of abuse of elderly people
by their caregivers, in the home. Most of the abuse goes
unreported because of the embarrassment and fear of reprisal
by the elderly people affected.

The victims are most likely to be female, aged 75 and up,
confused, and physically dependent. In the United States the
estimates of abuse cases range from half a million to 2.5
million per year.

The abuse is defined as physical abuse causing bodily
harm; verbal threats or psychological abuse causing fear or
humiliation; financial abuse of money or property; sexual
abuse as in rape or attempted rape; or neglect where food,
medication, medical treatment or supervision is not provided.

It is an emotional subject for both the public and the
professionals involved and strikes yet another blow at our
myth of tender, loving, family systems. We find it upsetting
to hear about and so contradictory to our value systems of
compassion and support for the elderly and handicapped that
there is danger of over-sensationalizing it. The web of
causes and effects will take some time to untangle, and we
are warned that we do not yet have reliable data, empirically
proven theories or even scientifically useful definitions
(Pedrick-Cornell and Gelles, 1982). We have, however, sufficient information to make it clear that abuse of the elderly
generally is not a crime; rather it indicates a family in
need of help.

With the demise of the extended family, the care of an
elderly parent or relative can create great difficulty –

physical, emotional or financial – for those who undertake the responsibility. Dr M. Lezak in the *Journal of Clinical Psychiatry* puts it bluntly. 'One who has not cared for an ill, helpless, confused, old person may not comprehend the helplessness, rage and frustration involved.' The care-givers may feel trapped in a situation of indeterminate length, for which they have no experience, no coping skills, no choices, and no way out. Old and unresolved family con-flicts may be reactivated, and new conflicts based on the role reversal – the dependency of the parent on the child – may arise. The inability to resolve such conflicts can trigger frustration and resentment. Certainly communication can be thwarted, if it has ever existed, by misunderstandings over life-styles, child-rearing practices, household man-agement, and possibly complicated by the loss of speech or hearing in the older person.

The presence of even a beloved elderly person in the home can place great stress on marital or parent-child relation-ships. If the caregiver is single, either male or female, social relationships or even career may be sacrificed. Such personal stress factors may be compounded by chronic ill-ness, inadequate finances, crowded living quarters, and the lack of a support system to share the burdens. Chronic sub-stance abuse is often involved, as are personality traits such as impulsive behaviour or the need to control.

The first abuse episode may be triggered by a crisis and the ensuing guilt simply increases the stress level and the likelihood of further abuse. As the cycle continues, the caregiver's feelings of denial and defensiveness cause them to withdraw and the family unit becomes increasingly iso-lated. The abused person, seeing no alternative, may comply, with increasing withdrawal, humiliation, and hopelessness. The fear of reprisal, of being placed in greater jeopardy if they admit to what is happening, causes the abused to deny any interference from outsiders who may try to help.

As our population of elderly people increases, there is mounting pressure to discourage institutional placement, yet it is totally unrealistic to assume that all families are capable of handling the responsibility at home. A Rathbone-McCuan article states 'those professionals who now advocate that the family should assume a greater role must recognize that caring for an aged person may create major shifts in the functional equilibrium throughout the entire family system.'

The policy of maintaining our elderly at home challenges us as a society to develop the kinds of services that families need. We have made a good start in Canada with home nursing and home-maker care, Meals-on-Wheels, Daycare Centres, Stroke Clubs, Short-stay Assessment Centres, and a well organized system of volunteer help. Our increasing awareness of abuse cases, however, makes it plain that these are not enough.

Emergency interventions are available on a voluntary basis of course, but as yet no legal immunity exists in any province for professionals or others who may wish to offer help. In any case, service provisions that focus only on the fact of abuse and not on the contributing factors may only make the family situation worse. Where abuse is suspected, the case management requires skilful efforts to establish a trusting relationship with all members of the family, crisis counselling to reduce the stress, the provision of appropriate practical support, and ongoing counselling to restructure the family relationships. This may suggest a misleading parallel with child abuse protection services. In dealing with adults, two overriding principles must be heeded - the client's right to privacy and self-determination, and the least restrictive alternative to care.

Moving back to a preventive approach, we need to help families consider the potential problems of taking an aging person into their home. By way of anticipatory guidance, there are realistic issues to be faced in making an assessment based not only on feelings of responsibility and guilt. If the decision is to make the move then education about methods of care is needed, with open discussion and perhaps contracting about the expectations on both sides. Families may need information about the aging process and the dynamics of multi-generational households.

Our hard-pressed social services are far from adequate to this task at the present time, and it would be fraudulent to raise public expectation of such help. It is not too soon, however, to raise public awareness of the problem, and to solicit the support of legislators and policy makers through whose efforts adult protective legislation and appropriate community resources will be instituted.

Happily, the vast majority of older people who need help are receiving good care from their families and friends, but there is a serious problem for an unfortunate few and that problem demands our attention.

References

Lezak, Dr. Muriel D. *Journal of Clinical Psychiatry*, 1978,
    39:592
Pedrick-Cornell, Claire, and Richard J. Gelles. 'Elder
Abuse:
    The Status of Current Knowledge,' *Family Relations*, July
    1982
Rathbone-McCuan, Eloise. 'Elderly Victims of Family Violence
and Neglect,' *Social Casework*, May 1980

Reprinted by permission of the author, who published this
paper in the *Gerontology Association of British Columbia
Newsletter*, Volume 6(3), Spring 1983.

ABUSE OF THE ELDERLY: KNOWNS AND UNKNOWNS
BENJAMIN SCHLESINGER AND RACHEL ABER SCHLESINGER

> There is no organized group of elderly victims of
> fraud, abuse, maltreatment, and criminal behavior
> who band together, and demand justice and public
> action.
>
> J.I. Kosberg, 1983, XIII

Most Canadians have heard that the 'baby boom' of the
'fifties' has given way to an 'aged boom' in the 'eighties.'
Less well known, however, is the remarkable size and pace of
growth in the elderly population. (Stone and Fletcher, 1986)

An aging Canada

At the turn of the century, this country's 271,201 aged made
up only 5 per cent of the total population. By mid-century,
their numbers had passed the one million mark and their
share of the population had risen to 7.8 per cent. The 1981
Census counted 2,360,975 people 65 and older, or 9.7 per
cent of all Canadians. The most recent estimates, for 1984,
put the elderly at 2,556,000 - 10 per cent of the population.
  The elderly are forecast to reach 3.5 million or 12 per
cent of the population in 2001. By the year 2031, there will
be in the order of 6.6 million aged men and women who will
account for about 20 per cent of all Canadians - double
their current proportion.
  The aging of Canada's population is phenomenal. In 1901,
only one person in twenty was 65 or older. Today one in ten
is aged. Fifty years from now, one Canadian in five will be
elderly.
  The 1981 Census counted 883,230 men and women 75 years
and older. The over-75s could reach a million and a half by

2001 and three to four million by the year 2041. Their share
of the elderly population has increased steadily as well,
from 31 per cent in 1951 to 37 per cent in 1981 and a
projected 50 to 55 per cent by 2041.

Women

Another striking trend is the rapidly expanding population
of elderly women. In 1901, women accounted for 48.8 per cent
of persons 65 and older. Their proportion increased to 49.2
per cent in 1951, 51.5 per cent by 1961, 55.2 per cent in
1971 and 57.2 per cent in 1981. By 2001, six in every ten
aged Canadians will be women.

Life expectancy

In 1986, the life expectancy for a Canadian woman was 80
years, for a man 72.9 years. In 1996, it is expected that
for women it will rise to 88.6 years, for men to 75 years.

The aging stage of family life

The final stage of the family life cycle begins with the
man's retirement, goes through the loss of the first spouse,
and ends with the death of the second. Because women live
longer than men and usually are younger than their husbands,
they are more often widowed than are men.
   The aging family stage begins with two persons, the
husband and wife, and ends with one, the surviving spouse.
The aging couple continue to be 'family' to their grown
children, grandchildren, and great-grandchildren.
   Family development continues through the final stage of
the family life cycle in the interaction of the family
members. An aging pair's developmental tasks are intertwined
now that they face the rest of life together. Both seek
mutually satisfactory answers to such questions as where
they will live, and on what, and how they will relate to one
another and to the other important people in their lives.
Both husband and wife now face the common task of developing
a life-style that will be meaningful to both. Each must
adjust to his or her declining health and strength and to
that of the other member of the pair.
   In time, one spouse dies and leaves the other widowed.
Most older couples continue on together for as long as they

both live, carrying out during the final stage of the family life cycle their joint family developmental tasks.

The elderly as resources

Television, newspapers, and popular magazines portray the old as a frail, dependent group that represents a drain on national and family resources. Recent research and policy debates have tended to emphasize the neediness and dependency of the old, depicting them as a drain on scarce resources. Yet there is a striking lack of perception of the old as constituting a resource - a lack that ignores economic as well as psychological realities.

With regard to the family realm, few systematic efforts have been made to map the flow of material support from older generations to the young, even though it is clear that the family is by far the most important welfare or redistributional mechanism even in an advanced industrial country like Canada. Available research evidence indicates that, overall, the old in Western industrialized societies tend to give more economic assistance than they receive.

We may have overlooked some critical functions performed by older generations. When families make plans, for example, regarding major purchases, they often count on the older generation as a potential backup if a crisis should intervene. Most older people own property, while it is becoming increasingly difficult for the young to do so. Often, the young may not actually end up turning to their elders, but their choices and behaviour would have been more restrained if the older generation were not there as potential support. Such functions of the older generations may constitute an important and much neglected aspect of modern grandparenthood.

Evidence shows that grandparents may serve as indirect 'stabilizers' of family life in a variety of ways. As a result of the clearer separation between parenthood and grandparenthood in the life of women, mothers may become more of a supportive force for their daughter's mothering. Grandparents may help to render parents more understandable to their children, may function as arbitrators in conflicts between them, or may serve as confidants in difficult times. Recently, writers have pointed to two particular current social trends that are likely to activate grandparents as stress-buffers: the growing number of single

adolescent parents and the high rates of divorce. In these
cases, grandparents may take over some of the tasks of
parenting. How often divorce leads to three-generational
living, and how often grandparents provide substantial
financial support to grandchildren following divorce, is not
known.

The elderly in the 21st century

The diversity, complexity, and importance of family relations in later life can be expected to become even greater
in the future. By 2000, the number of persons sixty-five and
over will increase even more. When today's young adults
reach old age, they will comprise at least 20 per cent of
the population. As social institutions take over more aspects
of life, such as income maintenance and health care, the
family may become even more important in providing lasting
emotional ties, a sense of identity, and a sense of self-
worth.

With the lengthening life span, couples may have thirty
to forty years ahead after the children leave home. Four-
and five-generation families will become common. More 'young
old' couples at retirement age with diminishing resources
will be involved in caring for their 'old old' parents. The
growing number of blended families through divorce and
remarriage will enlarge and complicate the extended family
network. On the other hand is the trend toward having fewer
or no children. The implications of nonparenthood for later
life adjustment are unknown and warrant study given the
significant role of children and grandchildren in the
resolution of later life tasks.

Because people are living longer than their elders did in
the past, we lack role models for later life family relations
just as we lack appropriate labels and role definitions. The
term 'post-parental' is unfortunate, for parents never cease
to be parents. Instead, it is the nature of parent-child
relationships that changes in later life. We are only beginning to explore the possibilities in that transformation.

Mark Novak, a Canadian sociologist in his book *Successful
Aging*, ends up his book by stating (Novak, 1985: 298):

In the past researchers too often studied the hardships
of old age. For every one account of good aging, volumes
and volumes of studies exist describing the misery of old
age. The lack of balance points to our deep prejudice
and fear of aging, and as long as we look only at sick

and troubled people and at the problems that come with
age, we shall never create an ideal of good aging to
which we can all aspire.

Today we can fulfil the basic needs of most older
people in our society, and more people than ever before
have the chance to live to a good old age. We can now
work to create the best possible old age, and there is
no better place to begin than with ourselves.

Abuse of the elderly

The issue of elder abuse emerged in the American literature
in the late 1970s (Steinmetz, 1978; Lau and Kosberg, 1979).
As the decade of the 1980s proceeded, the amount of attention increased in the North American literature on the topic
(Hudson, 1986).
   Kosberg (1983: XIII) points out that there is a growing
awareness about the victimization of the elderly. Such
adversity includes crime on the street and in the home by
strangers, maltreatment within institutional settings, fraud
and deception, and abuse by informal care providers. While
only a relatively small per cent of the elderly have been
victimized, fear, anxiety, and suspicion are fairly common
reactions by an elderly person. Unfortunately, victimization
of the elderly is often invisible to the general public.
Victimization can occur within homes, within institutions,
on crowded and busy streets, and through the mail. Individuals are the victims and only periodically does publicity
reach the general public.
   Elder abuse is part of the violation of rights that
encompass denial of basic rights of the aged person. These
rights include (Beck and Ferguson, 1981):

1. Having basic necessities met, such as food and decent
   housing.
2. Feeling useful and respected.
3. Having adequate medical care.
4. Obtaining employment based on merit.
5. Sharing in the community's recreational and
   educational resources.
6. Having moral and financial support from the family
   and community.
7. Having access to knowledge on how to improve later
   life and the resources that enable improvement, and
8. Living and dying with dignity.

Definition
The literature has difficulty in finding a uniform definition of elder abuse. We have chosen the definition of Health
and Welfare Canada (1986) as one which may be suitable.

ELDER ABUSE: may include the infliction of physical
injury, restraint, financial exploitation, threats,
ridicule, insult or humiliation, forced isolation
(physical or social), or forced change in living
arrangement.

ELDER NEGLECT: is the refusal or failure to care for the
older person whether intentional or unintentional (i.e.,
laziness or inadequate knowledge). This could include
abandonment, withholding or non-provision of food, health
care, companionship or assistance.

Types of elderly abuse
Giordano and Giordano (1984) point out the following six
categories of elderly abuse (pp. 232-233).

1. *Physical Abuse*. Physical abuse is violence that results
   in bodily harm or mental distress. It includes assault,
   unjustified denial of another's rights, sexual abuse,
   restrictions on freedom of movement, and murder.
2. *Negligence*. Negligence is the breach of duty or care-
   lessness that results in injury or the violation of
   rights.
3. *Financial exploitation*. Financial exploitation involves
   the theft or conversion of money or objects of value
   belonging to an elderly person by a relative or caretaker. It can be accomplished by force or through mis-
   representation.
4. *Psychological Abuse*. Psychological abuse is the provoking of the fear of violence or isolation, including name
   calling and other forms of verbal assault and threats of
   placement in a nursing home. It can be a spontaneous or
   protracted and systematic effort to dehumanize and
   usually is accompanied by other types of abuse.
5. *Violation of Rights*. The violation of rights is the
   breaching of rights that are guaranteed to all citizens
   by the Constitution, federal statutes, federal courts,
   and the states.
6. *Self-neglect*. Self-neglect includes self-inflicted
   physical harm and the failure to take care of one's
   personal needs. It stems from the elderly person's

diminished physical or mental abilities and is brought on
by the attitudes and behaviour of relatives.

We have expanded their categories in Table 1, to include
the various types of abuse found in our search of the
literature.

The categories in Table 1 represent some of the detailed
abuses which the elderly face in our society.

TABLE 1
Types of elder abuse by categories

Physical abuse

Beatings	Bruises, welts	Bone fractures
Lack of personal care	Dislocations	
Lack of food	Abrasions	
Lack of medical care	Lacerations	
Lack of supervision	Cuts, punctures	

Psychological abuse	Financial abuse
Verbal assault	Theft of money or property
Threat	Misuse of money or property
Fear	Poor residential environment
Isolation	

Criminal victimization

Purse snatching	Real estate deals	Funeral abuses
Consumer fraud	Nursing home fraud	Hearing aids
Confidence games	Home repairs	Pension fraud
Medical quackery	Car repairs	Insurance fraud

Institutional abuse

Theft of funds of patient
Costs unrelated to patient care
Duplicate payments from Health Insurance
Cutting expenses for the patient
Fraudulent therapy charges
Fraudulent pharmaceutical charges

Sexual abuse

Rape
Fondling
Touching
Molesting

A main factor which distinguishes abuse from other crimes is that it is committed by a caregiver, often an individual the older person loves and trusts. Thus, not only is it often not reported, but when it is reported the older person may deny it is happening. Many older people feel that to admit to being abused by one of their children is to admit to a major deficiency in themselves. This makes abuse difficult to document and even more difficult to resolve. Although the police can now lay charges in cases of domestic violence, such charges may lose credibility if the victim consistently denies the incident.

Abuse does occur in institutions as well as at home. Again there is not much documentation because frequently the abused patient does not complain or report, for any number of reasons including over-medication, fear of reprisal or inability to articulate the situation. As well, professionals may not recognize the abuse in the institutions.

Profile of the abused (Quinn and Tomita, 1986; 31)

From the existing research, Quinn and Tomita developed the following profile. They caution however that we have to consider other variables in future investigations:

> The population most at risk appears to be women over 75 years of age who are widows and, in most instances, reside with relatives, one of whom is the abuser. The elderly woman is most often white, is of poor to modest financial means, and is a Protestant. She is frail and vulnerable. Unlike abused children, who grow stronger with time, the abused elder will grow more dependent – with the abuse becoming even more likely. The typical abuser is presumably a caregiver because most victims clearly suffer from a range of physical and mental impairments. For victims of elder abuse and neglect, the abuser who also does caregiving may be all that stands between them and nursing home placement. The abuser is most frequently an adult child. It is not yet clear whether the usual abuser is a son or a daughter; the studies vary on this, although most tend to implicate the son and other males more heavily. The abuser is middle-aged unless he is a spouse or a grandchild. The abuse incidents are ongoing and can be expected to continue.

Casual factors (Health and Welfare, 1986)

The following are some of the factors underlying abuse of
the elderly:

> *The pathological framework*: views abusive behaviour as
> being determined solely by the personal or pathological
> problems of the abuser. Alcoholism, drug abuse, schizo-
> phrenia, and sociopathic behaviour all fall under this
> category as possible explanations for elder abuse.

> *The environmental framework*: views present situations
> and social conditions as being determinant of abusive
> behaviour.

> *The development framework*: views domestic violence as a
> learned behaviour which is passed on from generation to
> generation through established behaviour patterns.

For a complete discussion of theoretical backgrounds in
family violence consult the chapter by Gelles and Straus
(1979), and the review by Steinmetz (1978a).

Relevant factors in elder abuse (Project Share, 1981: 12-14)

Some of the factors to be considered in abuse of the elderly
are:
1. *Retaliation*: Some surmise that elderly abuse is a form
of retaliation or revenge. There may be unresolved conflicts
and resentments existing between parent and child which come
to a head again when they are in the same home, according to
a theory offered by the Chronic Illness Center in Cleveland,
Ohio. This may be compounded if the elderly parent continues
to bait the child. Also, there may be a symbiotic relationship where the parent and child are mutually dependent on
one another. The aging parent may threaten or cut off money
or support from his or her adult child which will trigger
anger, resentment, and abuse, particularly when the adult
has been drinking.
2. *Ageism and violence as a way of life*: Another
rationale for elderly abuse is thought by some to be the
widespread acceptance of violence in American society. In
some families, patterns of violence exist from generation to

generation as a normal response to stress. This, combined with the negative attitudes society generally holds towards the aged, can increase their likelihood of abuse.

3. *Lack of close family ties*: In some families where there are no close ties, the sudden appearance of a dependent elderly parent can precipitate stress and frustration without the love and friendship necessary to counteract the new responsibilities of the adult children. In some cases, the parent may be reunited with children after many years of separation.

4. *Lack of financial resources*: The pressures and frustration of family and financial problems is often cited by experts as a factor which drives family members to abusive behaviour. The families may contribute a great deal of support to home maintenance, health care and other needs of their elderly members. Adding to a potentially already tense financial situation is the factor that women, the primary caregivers in families, are increasingly involved in the workforce. If the older person requires supervision or assistance, she may be forced to give up her job, further reducing the family paycheque.

Services such as day care, respite care, and home health may not be available even if the family could afford them. Many believe that it is this inability to obtain needed services, coupled with a lack of financial resources, which can build resentment and foster an atmosphere conducive to abuse.

5. *Resentment of dependency*: Often children or relatives may wish to do 'the right thing,' but they are unable to cope with the resulting financial and emotional stress. They are often faced with multiple responsibilities to spouses, children, and grandchildren. The 'child' may be in her fifties or sixties and have diminished strength to cope with the care of aging parents on a 24-hour basis. The situation may be one where one person (the caregiver) is putting her life on hold, spending all day, every day, as the sole companion of a person who may need almost constant attention. Caring for a frail elderly patient who requires a considerable amount of assistance can be very draining.

The older person also may resent his or her dependency and become either more aggressive or withdrawn, which may also be a source of aggravation for the abuser.

6. *Increased life expectancy*: There has been a dramatic increase in the numbers of persons reaching age 75 and over. This is the fastest growing segment of the population. This

is also a population more likely to require care. As a result of medical advances and other reasons, the dependency period of old age has been extended. The period of care may be for a long duration.

7. *Lack of community resources*: Even the best of parent-child relationships can deteriorate as the burden of care persists over a long period of time. Those children who are financially equipped to maintain their dependent relatives in their homes often times are unable to find the services in their communities to assist them to do so. Few support systems currently exist in local communities for caregivers to draw upon and those that do exist are virtually unknown to the average citizen. Some experts see abuse of the elderly as a natural consequence of inadequate services to families caring for a frail elderly relative.

8. *Stress and other life crises*: The dramatic change that can occur when a frail elderly parent moves in with a family already struggling in several areas of family relationships produces intense stress. For some elderly, constant supervision is necessary. Most experts agree that family stress is a major precipitating factor in elderly abuse. One study found that the family claimed the elderly person as a significant source of stress in 63 per cent of the reported abuse cases.

9. *History of personal or mental problems*: In families where the adult child has a history of personal pathological problems, a potential for abuse exists. In numerous individual cases, mentally impaired children were responsible for abusing their parents.

10. *History of alcohol and drug abuse*: There are many instances of abuse wherein the abuser was experiencing alcohol and drug consumption problems. Substance abuse is readily identifiable as contributing to, if not causing, family violence.

11. *Environmental conditions*: Quality of housing, unemployment, family conflict, substance abuse, and crowded neighbourhoods and living conditions can precipitate stress and lead to violence singly or in combination with other factors.

Incidence

At this time we do not have precise statistics related to elder abuse. The estimates in the United States are that about 3.2 per cent or 2.5 million elderly are abused. In

Canada 2-4 per cent of the senior citizens, amounting to
more than 100 000 per year are the victims of abuse (Shell,
1982).

Intervention

As far as intervention is concerned, Bookin and Dunkle
(1985:12) state:

> Successful intervention in the area of elder abuse will
> also require the development of new helping techniques,
> rather than the simple transference of skills used in
> working with other client populations or elderly clients
> with other types of problems. The elderly, frequently
> left out of case plans utilizing family therapy, should
> be considered as an integral part in treatment.

Sengstock, Barrett and Graham (1984) add some other
suggestions for dealing with elderly abuse (p. 111). Their
multi-faceted approach includes:

1. Crisis intervention techniques and provision of
   protective shelters for the victim, if necessary.
2. Counselling for the abuser is necessary to assist
   him/her in dealing with frustration and problems through
   less destructive means.
3. Alleviation of the general family problems suffered by
   victim and abuser alike must be accomplished. This
   requires that services of all types - economic assistance, employment counselling, medical care, as well as
   general counselling - be easily available.

Prevention

As pointed out by Podnieks (1985), prevention is crucial.
She suggests five ways of deterring abuse:

- Reversing our society's approval and promotion of
  violence in the community and at home.
- Using all possible means to reduce stresses within
  families because these are the forerunners of violence
  and abuse.
- Facilitating meaningful relationships between families
  and their neighbours and communities to counteract the
  isolated existence of so many.

- Changing the balance of power, decision-making and
  sharing of household tasks to alleviate the gross
  inequalities with discrimination toward elderly and
  women.
- Interrupting the historical patterns of violence in
  generations of families.

These steps are essentially aimed at the roots of family
violence and lay the groundwork for decreasing the future
incidence.

The professional and abuse of the elderly

Bookin and Dunkle (1985) discuss the problems which workers
face in dealing with elderly abuse. They include the following areas:

a) It may be quite difficult to identify elderly abuse.
b) What is the definition of abuse in each community and
   cultural group?
c) What are the laws related to elderly abuse?
d) How does one get access to cases, when most elderly
   persons will not report abuse?
e) How does one consider the family stresses involved in
   elderly abuse?
f) The worker will have to deal with the whole family
   system not only the abused.
g) Frequently the abused elderly react with denial, resigna-
   tion, withdrawal, fear or depression. This will have
   to be dealt with by the worker.
h) Feelings of guilt, shame, helplessness and worthlessness
   are also associated by the abused elderly person.

Legislation

At the present time, in Canada there is little legislation
or a procedure for dealing with elder abuse. The Manitoba
Council on Aging has taken the first steps towards defining
the problem and recommending means of dealing with elder
abuse. Their report stressed the need for the following
methods of intervention (Shell, 1982):

1. Prevention
2. Education of professionals, caregivers and the general
   public
3. A protection system

Although all three methods are important, Canada has only begun the education process. And even with the protective legislation, adequate services must be provided to create a protective system.

The United States has protective legislation in many jurisdictions. Connecticut is considered to have the model system with mandatory reporting statutes plus support services. Their system includes an Ombudsman Office. Trained

volunteer patient advocates work in long-term care facilities, reporting any suspected abuse to the Regional Ombudsman. The Ombudsman investigates complaints of abuse submitted by the volunteer advocates and from the community. An important part of the Connecticut system is the provision of counselling and support services. Although services are not generally imposed on the abused senior, Connecticut does have guardianship legislation which allows a temporary guardian to be appointed by the court, if necessary.

The Connecticut experience points to the need for mandatory reporting legislation. Prior to the legislation, there was little motivation for keeping records. In the first year following the adoption of legislation, the Ombudsman's Office investigated 700 referrals.

Some knowns

In reviewing the existing knowledge on the topic, Pedrick-Cornell and Gelles (1982) and Giordano and Giordano (1984) find the following trends (in the United States).

a) *Incidence*: It is estimated that one in ten elderly persons living with relatives is abused each year.
b) *Victims*: The majority of victims are women and men who have a physical/mental disability.
c) *Type of Abuse*: Psychological abuse is more common than physical abuse.
d) *The Abusers*: In 90 per cent of the cases the abuser is a relative. Daughters are the abusers twice as often as any other relative followed by sons, granddaughters, husbands and siblings.

Other trends were noted by Walker (1983).

1. Abuse occurs in rural, suburban and urban areas.
2. Abuse occurs in all economic groups.

3. The majority of the clients are 80 or older.
4. Advanced age, alcoholism, and psychiatric problems
   appear to influence the family member's handling of an
   elder person.

The unknowns

Some of the unknowns have been pointed out by Hudson
(1986: 125-166).
1. What are the boundaries of elder abuse, elder neglect,
   self-abuse and exploitation. We seem to have varied
   definitions related to abuse of the elderly.
2. Is elder abuse a legal problem or a criminal act.
3. What type of public education do we need related to
   elder abuse.
4. How can the mass media help to focus our attention on
   elder abuse without hysteria.

From our review of the literature some additional
'unknowns' emerged.

1. What type of training do professionals require to deal
   with abuse of the elderly.
2. What kind of treatment is available for the abusers.
3. How can institutions for the elderly implement prevention
   programs against abuse.
4. What is a good legal code to protect the elderly from
   abuse.

We have just touched the tip of the iceberg in examining
and identifying abuse of the elderly. We believe that there
are more 'unknowns' than 'knowns,' and as one examines the
present studies on the topic one gets the feeling that there
is a long road ahead in this important area of human concern.

Research questions

Hudson (1986: 161) poses thirteen questions for future
research related to elder abuse.

1. How are elder care decisions made and by whom?
2. What factors affect the making of such decisions so
   that the decision is appropriate to the individuals
   involved?

3. What are the effects of family elder care on the nuclear family unit, the primary caregiver, and the care-receiving elder?
4. What are the antecedents and consequences of elder abuse? Elder neglect? Exploitation? Self-neglect? Multiple abuse and neglect?
5. Are there differences in the abuser and/or victim in different types of elder mistreatment?
6. What forms and type of support do elder caregiving families most need and want? What about care-receiving elders?
7. Are there ethnic/cultural or socioeconomic differences with regard to elder mistreatment?
8. How do the various service and health care professionals respond to and intervene with families doing elder care and with abusive family situations?
9. How can existing elder care resources be allocated to maximize effective utilization?
10. What barriers deter effective identifications of and interventions for family elder care issues and elder mistreatment situations?
11. Do the dynamics and causes vary with different elder mistreatment situations? For example, how much of elder abuse is spouse abuse, how much is child abuse revisited on the elder, and how much of it is a distinct phenomenon?
12. What are the most specific and sensitive signs and symptoms of the various forms of elder mistreatment?
13. What is the relationship between alcohol abuse and elder mistreatment?

Conclusion

Elder abuse in the 1980s is a complex problem. We are just beginning to delve into the myriad of factors in our society which play a part in this phenomenon. It is only a decade, since the first published articles and studies appeared in North America. We leave the last word to Schlesinger (1984: 59):

We must be aware of the crime of elderly abuse, and we must begin to initiate programs and attitudes to prevent it. We support rape-crisis centres, we fight to help the battered wife, and we speak out against child abuse in all forms. We fight for quality of life. Why are we silent when our mothers and grandmothers struggle alone and in silence in their battle for survival, for growing old in an atmosphere of dignity and understanding? We must provide the strength for those who no longer have much strength. We must hear the silent cries, and our voices must help them speak. We too will grow old, and we too want to live in a world of mutual respect, love, and care, not increased elderly abuse, not a world of 'granny-bashing.'

References

Beck, C.M. and D. Ferguson. 'Aged Abuse,' *Journal of Gerontological Nursing* 7 (June 1981): 333-6

Bookin, D. and R.E. Dunkle. 'Elder Abuse: Issues for the Practitioner,' *Social Casework* 66 (Jan. 1985): 3-12

Gelles, R. and M.A. Straus. 'Determinants of Violence in the Family: Toward a Theoretical Integration,' (in) W.R. Burr et al., eds. *Contemporary Theories About the Family*, Vol. I. New York: The Free Press, 1979, 549-81.

Giordano, N. and J. Giordano. 'Elder Abuse: A Review of the Literature,' *Social Work* 29 (May-June 1984): 232-6

Health and Welfare Canada. *Abuse and Neglect of the Elderly.* Ottawa: Health and Welfare Canada, National Clearinghouse on Family Violence, 1986.

Hudson, M.F. 'Elder Mistreatment: Current Research,' (in) Pillemer, K.A. and R.S. Wolf, eds. *Elder Abuse: Conflict in the Family.* Dover, Mass.: Auburn House, 1986, 125-66

Lau, E. and J.I. Kosberg. 'Abuse of the Elderly by Informal Caregivers,' *Aging* 2 (Sept.-Oct. 1979): 10-15

Novak, M. *Successful Aging.* Markham, Ont.: Penguin Books, 1985

Pedrick-Cornell and R. Gelles. 'Elder Abuse: The Status of Current Knowledge,' *Family Relations* 31 (July 1982): 457-65

Podnieks, E. 'Abuse of the Elderly: When Caregivers Cease to Care,' *Perspectives* 9 (Winter 1985), 10-12

Project Share. 'Abuse of the Elderly,' *Human Services.* Monograph No. 27, September 1981

Schlesinger, R. 'Granny Bashing,' *Canadian Woman Studies* 5 (Spring 1984): 56-9

Sengstock, M.C., Barrett, S. and R. Graham. 'Abused Elders: Victims of Villains or of Circumstances?' *Journal of Gerontological Social Work* 8 (Fall-Winter 1984): 101-11

Shell, D. *Protection of the Elderly: A Study of Elder Abuse*. Winnipeg, Man.: Manitoba Association of Gerontology, 1982

Steinmetz, S. 'Battered Parents,' *Society* 15 (July–Aug. 1978): 54–5

-- 'Violence between Family Members,' *Marriage and Family Review* 1 (May–June 1978): 1–16 (a)

Stone, L.O. and S. Fletcher. *The Seniors Boom*. Ottawa: Minister of Supply and Services, 1986, Catalogue No. 89–515

Walker, J.C. 'Protective Services for the Elderly: Connecticut's Experience,' (in) Kosberg, J.I., ed. *Abuse and Maltreatment of the Elderly: Causes and Intervention*. Boston: John Wright, PSG Inc., 1983, 292–302

ANNOTATED BIBLIOGRAPHY

Abstracts on aging

1. Costa, J.J. 'Abstracts, Indexes, Periodicals, Journals'
   (in) J.J. Costa, ed. *Abuse of the Elderly*,
   1984, 195–224
   Adresses of journals related to content on elderly
   abuse are noted in this section of the book.

Agencies dealing with abuse

2. Costa, J.J. 'State and Area Agencies on Aging' (in)
   J.J. Costa, ed. *Abuse of the Elderly*, 1984, 99–170
   The addresses of agencies of all the States in the
   United States who deal with aging are included in
   Chapter 8 of the book.

3. Johnson, T.F., O'Brien, J.G., and Hudson, M.F. 'A
   Directory of Organizations Providing Services to Older
   Persons.' (in) *Elder Neglect and Abuse: An Annotated
   Bibliography*, (by the authors). Westport, Connecticut:
   Greenwood Press, 1985, 171–99.
   The addresses of American State Adult Protection
   Services, State Aging Services, State Medicaid
   Agencies, State Mental Health Services, and National
   Organizations.

Aging: assessment

4. Ferguson, D. and Beck, C. 'H.A.L.F. – A Tool to Assess
   Elder Abuse Within the Family,' *Geriatric Nursing*,
   Vol. 4 (Sept.–Oct. 1983), 301–4.
   A method to assess elder abuse.

5. Hwalek, M. and Sengstock, M.C. 'Developing an Index of
   Elder Abuse: Final Report.' Detroit: Institute of
   Gerontology, Wayne State University, April 1, 1985.
   Describes the development of two indices for identifying victims of elder abuse and neglect. Discusses the
   need for such indices, and addresses psychometric
   issues. Assesses existing measures for the identification of elder abuse. The Hwalek-Sengstock Risk
   Assessment Tool is a 17-time screening instrument for
   identifying at-risk elderly. The Sengstock-Hwalek Comprehensive Index of Elder Abuse is a 19-page instrument
   for the systematic documentation of the presence of six
   categories of elder abuse or neglect. The latter index
   can also reveal whether the abuse is intentional;
   determine if self-abuse or self-neglect is involved;
   and provide information on demographic characteristics
   of the victim as well as information about the service
   provider.

6. Sengstock, M., Hwalek, M., and S. Moshier. 'A
   Comprehensive Index for Assessing Abuse and Neglect of
   the Elderly.' (in) M.W. Galbraith ed. *Convergence in
   Aging*, 1986, 41-64.
   A description of the Sengstock-Hwalek Comprehensive
   Index of Elder Abuse. Includes some case studies.

Aging: background

7. Bengtson, V. and E. DeTerre. 'Aging and Family
   Relations,' *Marriage and Family Review* 3 (Spring/Summer
   1980), 51-76.
   A review of the literature related to family support
   for the aged.

8. Brubaker, T.H. ed. *Family Relationships in Later
   Life*. Beverly Hills, California: Sage, 1983.
   Fourteen papers examine the complexities of family
   relationships of the aged in the United States.

9. Canadian Journal on Aging. Gerontological Trends and
   Issues in Social Welfare. *Canadian Journal on Aging*, 6
   (Summer 1987), Special Issue.
   Six papers discuss various aspects of aging related to
   social welfare issues.

10. Daedalus. 'The Aging Society,' *Daedalus*, 115 (Winter 1986) Special Issue.
    Seventeen contributers write about inter-disciplinary aspects of the American aging society.

11. Driedger, L. and N. Chappell. *Aging and Ethnicity: Toward an Interface*. Toronto: Butterworths, 1987.
    A review of the research and policy literature on aging and ethnicity in Canada.

12. Family Coordinator. Aging in a Changing Family Context: Special Issue. *Family Coordinator*, 27 (October, 1978), 301-504.
    This special issue deals with all aspects related to aging in the United States in the late 1970's.

13. Marshall, V.W., ed. *Aging in Canada: Social Perspectives*. Toronto: Fitzhenry and Whiteside, 1987. 2nd edition.
    Thirty papers cover varied aspects of aging in Canada, including family structure and social relationships (pp. 262-394).

14. Gee, E.M. and M.M. Kimball. *Women and Aging*. Toronto: Butterworths, 1987.
    A sociologist and a psychologist highlight the significant relationship between aging and women's issues.

15. McDaniel, S.A. *Canada's Aging Population*. Toronto: Butterworths, 1986.
    Presents the present demographic trends related to Canada's aging population.

16. Ragan, P.K. ed. *Aging Parents*. Los Angeles: University of Southern California, 1979.
    Twenty papers discuss varied aspects related to aged parents, including family related issues.

17. Stone, L.O. and S. Fletcher. *The Seniors Boom*. Ottawa: Minister of Supply and Service, 1986. Catalogue No. 89-515.
    A statistical analysis of the elderly in Canada.

Bibliographies

18. Carrière, R. and A. Thomson. eds. *Family Violence: A Bibliography of Ontario Resources, 1980-1984*. Sudbury, Ontario: Laurentian University, 1985.
Part 4 contains items on elder abuse (pp. 65-67).

19. Costa, J.J. 'Bibliography on Elder Abuse,' (in) J.J. Costa ed. *Abuse of the Elderly*, 1984, 225-90.
A comprehensive bibliography on elder abuse which contains many items related to crime and the elderly.

20. Family Violence Research Program, University of Texas at Tyler. *Spousal Abuse: A Reference List*, 1986.
Includes a bibliography of over 700 published and unpublished articles related to spousal abuse through December 1986.

21. Grant, M. 'Abuse of the Aged: A Bibliography of Crane Library Holdings.' Toronto: Crane Library, 1985.
The J.W. Crane Memorial Library is a facility of the Canadian Geriatrics Research Society, a private non-profit organization located at 351 Christie Street, Toronto, Ontario M6G 3C3. This bibliography contains largely journal articles and special reports 1975-1985 – thirty three articles and 12 monographs.

22. Hawley, D.L. ed. *Women and Aging: A Comprehensive Bibliography*. Vancouver: Simon Fraser University, The Gerontology Research Centre, 1985.
Family issues related to women and aging (pp. 1-23) are included in this bibliography.

23. Johnson, T.F., O'Brien, J.G. and M.F. Hudson. *Elder Neglect and Abuse: An Annotated Bibliography*, Westport CT.: Greenwood Press, 1985.
This bibliography presents 144 annotated and 205 un-annotated references on elder neglect and abuse. The annotated entries emphasize elder abuse in family settings, while unannotated entries focus on elder mistreatment in family and in nonfamily settings. The annotated section includes literature on elder mistreatment written since 1975, in the form of empirical research, reviews, reports, hearings, conference pro-ceedings, training guides, detection instruments,

unpublished manuscripts, and a variety of theoretical, policy, and discussion papers. Each annotated citation specifies the professional orientation of the first author, the type of exposition used, the substantive issues mentioned in the entry, citation information, and the annotation, which includes the topic, objectives, methods, findings, and conclusions. The unannotated section contains a selected professional bibliography, newspapers and media sources. A model Adult Protective Services Act is also included (pp. 201-219).

24. Kemmer, E. *Violence in the Family: An Annotated Bibliography*. New York: Garland Press, 1984. This bibliography contains 1055 items on family violence (1960-1982), including historical perspectives.

25. National Clearinghouse on Family Violence. An Annotated Bibliography on Elder Abuse. *Vis à Vis* 1(Autumn 1983), 2-3. A small annotated bibliography on elder abuse up to 1983.

26. Quinn, M.J. *Elder Abuse Bibliography*. San Francisco: Consortium for Elder Abuse Prevention, 1986. Contains more than 150 entries from published and unpublished books, journals, reports, and articles.

Booklets

27. University of New Hampshire. *Elder Abuse and Neglect: Recommendations from the Research Conference on Elder Abuse and Neglect*. Durham, N.H., Family Research Laboratory, June 1986. A 15-page booklet which contains recommendations of a Research Conference of 30 participants.

28. Milt, H. *Family Neglect and Abuse of the Aged: A Growing Concern*. New York: Public Affairs Pamphlet, No. 603, 1982. An examination of elder abuse by family members in popular language. The problems of dealing with elder abuse are also included.

29. Project Share. *Abuse of the Elderly. Human Services*, Monograph Series, No. 27, September 1981.

A summary of elder abuse in the U.S.A., including available studies up to 1981.

Books

30. Anetzberger, G.J. *The Etiology of Elder Abuse by Adult Offspring.* Springfield, Illinois; Charles C. Thomas, 1987.
A discussion of physical abuse of elderly parents. The book analyzes interviews of filial caregivers.

31. Costa, J.J. ed. *Abuse of the Elderly: A Guide to Resources and Services.* Toronto: D.C. Heath (Lexington Books). 1984.
A compilation of articles and resources related to elder abuse.

32. Galbraith, M. ed. 'Elder Abuse: Perspectives on our Emerging Crisis,' *Convergence in Aging* 3(1986).
Written for a broad audience of practitioners, policy-makers, and academicians, this volume provides back-ground on the problem of abuse and neglect among community-dwelling elderly and how it has been addressed in research, policy and practice.

33. Kosberg, J.I. (ed.). *Abuse and Maltreatment of the Elderly; Causes and Interventions.* Boston: John Wright PSG Inc., 1983.
This book presents a multidisciplinary approach to the problem of elder abuse. It outlines the extent of victimization among the elderly within the practical experience and original research of 34 contributors. Objectives are to determine the reasons for elder abuse, to identify particularly vulnerable groups with-in the elderly population and to propose new strategies for professionals dealing with the problem.

34. Pagelow, M.D. and L.W. Pagelow. *Family Violence,* New York. Praeger, 1984.
Most Americans cling to an image of the family that includes tranquility, happiness, love between members, shared norms and values, and above all else, safety. Recent investigations, however, have been making it increasingly clear that the home is a dangerous place: that more violent crimes occur in the home than outside

its doors, and that more violence occurs between family members than among strangers. Family violence is a cross-disciplinary work that brings together in one source many theoretical and empirical findings from scientific research on violent acts, actors, and victims. The author examines the difficulties involved in the study of family violence, especially the question of privacy, and discusses the extent of the problem in society. Various theories of family violence are introduced, together with the causes that have been cited to explain its occurrence.

35. Pillemer, K. and R.S. Wolf. eds. *Elder Abuse in the Family*, Dover, Mass: Auburn House, 1986.
This book of readings includes items on historical data, family neglect,caregiver burdens, current research reviews, definitions, findings from special studies, and treatment and prevention of elder abuse.

36. Quinn, M.J. and S.K. Tomita. *Elder Abuse and Neglect*. New York: Springer, 1986.
This book explores the nature of elder abuse, examines why and how older adults are abused, and provides guidelines for detection and effective intervention. Combining current theory with clinical practice, the authors discuss the many forms of abuse whether physical, psychological, or financial. Actual case examples from clinical experience show how abuse looks in the field. Detailed clinical protocols are included.

37. Yin, P. *Victimization of the Aged*. Springfield, Illinois: Charles C. Thomas, 1985.
The book discusses crime victimization of older persons. Includes a review of the literature.

Caregivers

38. Beck, C.M. and D. Ferguson. 'Aged Abuse,' *Journal of Gerontological Nursing*. 7(June 1981), 333-36.
This article is an attempt to fill the gap in the nursing literature concerning the abuse of elderly parents who reside with, and are dependent upon, their adult caretaking children. The phenomenon of abuse of the aged is examined within the framework of role theory; a change in the role of the elderly parent, and

a concomitant need for change in the adult child's role is seen as affecting the way aged parents are treated.

39. Beck, C.M. and L.R. Phillips, 'Abuse of the Elderly,' *Journal of Gerontological Nursing.* 9(Feb. 1983.), 97–101.
This article presents concepts for understanding why abuse may occur, especially when the dependent older person is confused. It describes behaviour that may be expected from a confused person and the responses these behaviours may elicit from the caregiver.

40. Caro, F.G. 'Relieving Informal Caregiver Burden through Organized Services.' (in) K.A. Pillemer and R.S. Wolf eds. *Elder Abuse: Conflict in the Family*, 1986, 283–96.
A discussion of the challenge facing our aging society and the role of family members in providing long-term care for their aged relatives.

41. Cicirelli, V.G. 'The Helping Relationship and Family Neglect in Later Life.' (in) K.A. Pillemer and R.S. Wolf eds. *Elder Abuse: Conflict in the Family*, 1986, 49–66.
An attempt to show how the dynamics of the helping relationship can help to explain neglect of the elderly by their adult child caregivers.

42. George, L.K. 'Caregiver Burden: Conflict between Norms of Reciprocity and Solidarity.' (in) K.A. Pillemer and R.S. Wolf eds. *Elder Abuse: Conflict in the Family*, 1986, 67–92.
A discussion of the caregiver burden that relates to the physical, psychological, financial and emotional problems of impaired adults.

43. Lau, E. and J.I. Kosberg, 'Abuse of the Elderly by Informal Care Providers,' *Aging.* (Sept./Oct. 1979), 10–15.
The authors describe an exploratory study of elder abuse conducted at the Chronic Illness Center in Cleveland, Ohio. A total of 39 cases of abuse were identified, representing 9.6 per cent of all elderly clients seen by the agency over one year. Theories

regarding abuse are discussed, as are possible interventions and the implications of such interventions
from the legal, practice, and policy viewpoints.

44. Steinmetz, S. 'Elder Abuse,' *Aging*. (Jan./Feb. 1981.)
6–10.
This study represents the first attempt to investigate
elder abuse by interviewing the caregiving children of
elderly parents. Using a snowball sampling technique, a
total of sixty in-depth interviews were conducted. The
data collected suggests that the use of verbal, emo-
tional/psychological, and physical control of the
elderly by their caregiving children is widespread. The
data is also analyzed in order to uncover some of the
dilemmas which caregiving children encounter while
caring for their elderly parents.

45. Steinmetz, S.K. and D.J. Amsden. 'Dependent Elders,
Family Stress, and Abuse.' (in) T.H. Brubaker
ed. *Family Relationships in Later Life*. Beverly Hills,
California: Sage, 1983, 173–92.
A study of 119 persons who were caregivers living with
and caring for an aged parent. Social/emotional and
mental health dependencies are the most stress and
violence producing.

46. Steinmetz, S.K. 'Dependency, Stress, and Violence
Between Middle-Aged Caregivers and their Elderly
Parents.' (in) J. Kosberg ed. *Abuse and Maltreatment of
the Elderly*, 1983, 134–49.
A discussion of the strains inherent in caring for a
growing number of the elderly in our population.

47. Steinmetz, S. 'Elder Abuse: One Fifth of Our Population
At Risk,' *Caring*, 5(January 1986) 69–71.
The risk that frail elders will be abused by over-
burdened family caregivers was discussed in testimony
presented to the House Select Committee on Aging in
May 1985. It was argued that, while adult children are
probably providing more care, and more humane care,
than at any other time in history, it cannot be assumed
that they will be able to continue to provide this care
without adequate resources and support systems. Recent
public policy changes that have resulted in reduced

social services, redefinitions of eligibility for many
services, and attempts to tighten state relative
responsibility laws are criticized.

48. Zdorkowski, R.T. 'Adult Caregivers and Their Perceptions
    of Caregiving.' (in) M.W. Galbraith ed. *Convergence in
    Aging*, 1986, 28-40.
    Case histories of adult caregivers and how they view
    their tasks.

Case studies

49. 'Impact of Long Term Sexual Abuse,' *Clinical
    Gerontologist* 4(April 1986) 47-50.
    This case-study describes the impact of incestuous
    abuse on a sixty-four year old women who had suffered
    from sexual abuse from an older male sibling from her
    childhood into middle-age.

50. Duenas, M.T. 'Impact of Long-Term Sexual Abuse,'
    Clinical Gerontologist 4(April 1986) 47-50.
    Case study of an elderly woman, aged 64, who had
    suffered long-term sexual abuse from her older male
    sibling until she was 52 years old. She was engaged in
    counselling with the author because of emotional and
    adjustment problems related to the abuse.

51. Gesino, J.P., H.H. Smith and W.A. Keckich. 'The
    Battered Woman Grows Old,' *Clinical Gerontologist*
    1(Fall 1982) 59-67.
    Cases of two battered older women, 73 and 76 years,
    admitted to a private psychiatric hospital for the
    treatment of despression are reported. The women
    refused to discuss the long history of physical or
    verbal abuse they had experienced from their spouses
    but did discuss their husbands' expectations of them
    and their expectations of themselves as marriage
    partners. Most of the information presented was
    obtained from interviews with their adult children.

52. Pillemer, K.A. 'Risk Factors in Elder Abuse: Results
    from a Case-Control Study.' (in) K.A. Pillemer and
    R.S. Wolf eds. *Elder Abuse: Conflict in the Family*,
    1986, 239-63.
    The findings from a case-control study that attempted
    to identify risk factors for physical elder abuse.

53. Rathbone-McCuan, E. 'Elderly Victims of Family Violence and Neglect,' *Social Casework*, 61(May 1980), 296-304. Through the use of ten case studies, this article describes and analyzes various situations in which non-institutionalized elderly persons become victims of non-accidental physical abuse and neglect by supposedly 'caring' persons. Techniques for intervention and the barriers encountered when implementing such strategies are discussed.

Causality

54. Anderson, L. and M. Thobahen. 'Clients in Crisis,' *Journal of Gerontological Nursing*. 10(December 1984) 6-10.
A summary of information regarding incidence and theories of causality of elder abuse, along with a description of the role of the nurse in assessment and intervention.

55. Douglass, R.L. and T. Hickey. 'Domestic Neglect and Abuse of the Elderly: Research Findings and a Systems Perspective for Service Delivery Planning.' (in) J. Kosberg ed. *Abuse and Maltreatment of the Elderly*, 1983, 115-33.
This chapter reviews early evidence about the causes of neglect and abuse of the elderly. The authors propose service delivery efforts to meet the present needs of the elderly.

56. Johnson, D. 'Abuse and Neglect - Not for Children Only,' *Journal of Gerontological Nursing*. 5(July/August 1979) 12-15.
This article looks at the relationships between child abuse and the abuse of the elderly. Several possible causes of elder abuse are discussed and a proposed model for elder abuse is put forth as a starting point for future study.

Crime against the elderly

57. Brillon, Y. *Victimization and Fear of Crime Among the Elderly*. Toronto: Butterworths, 1987. This book discusses research information from Canada and abroad (United States and Great Britain) on how crime affects the lives of senior citizens.

58. Clarke, A.H. 'Perceptions of Crime and Fear of
    Victimisation Among Elderly People,' *Aging and Society*,
    4(September 1984), 327–42.
    Most of the research into fear of crime among the
    elderly has been conducted in the United States of
    America particularly during the past ten years. This
    paper begins by summarising the major findings which
    have emerged from this work. Attention is then turned
    to similar studies which have recently been undertaken
    in Britain. The findings from a small sample survey of
    elderly residents in a town in the south of England are
    then reported.

59. Clemente, F. and M.B. Kleiman. 'Fear of Crime Among the
    Aged.' (in) J.J. Costa ed. *Abuse of the Elderly*, 1984,
    13–20.
    This chapter focuses on the fear of crime among older
    persons.

60. Finley, G.E. 'Fear of Crime in the Elderly.' (in)
    J. Kosberg ed. *Abuse and Maltreatment of the Elderly*,
    1983, 21–39.
    The author discusses four issues related to fear of
    crime in the elderly since the late 1960's.

61. Gubrium, J.F. 'Victimization in Old Age: Evidence and
    Three Hypotheses.' (in) J.J. Costa ed. *Abuse of the
    Elderly*, 1984, 25–32.
    Presents available data on rates of victimization among
    the elderly and develops hypotheses.

62. Jaycox, V.H. and L.J. Center. 'A Comprehensive Response
    to Violent Crimes Against Older Persons.' (in) J.
    Kosberg ed. *Abuse and Maltreatment of the Elderly*,
    1986, 316–34.
    An introduction to crime prevention and victim assist-
    ance service for seniors.

63. Kunkle, S. and J.A. Humphrey, 'Murder of the Elderly:
    An Analysis of Increased Vulnerability' *Omega* 13, No. 1
    (1982–1983) 27–34.
    This study investigates trends related to homicide
    victimization of the aged in the United States as a
    whole and in North Carolina in particular. Data on all
    officially recorded cases of homicide in North Carolina

among persons aged 60 and over from 1972 to 1977 form
the basis for analysis. Although available evidence
indicates that the aged are at low risk for most types
of crime, particularly violent offenses, rates for the
United States show that murder among the aged is rising
faster than among any other age group.

64. Liang, J. and M.C. Sengstock. 'Personal Crimes against
the Elderly.' (in) J. Kosberg ed. *Abuse and Maltreatment of the Elderly*, 1983, 40–67.
This chapter discusses criminal victimization of the
elderly in the U.S.A.

65. Orzek, A.M. and C. Loganbill. 'Treatment Strategies for
Fear of Crime among the Elderly,' *Clinical
Gerontologist*, 4(January 1985), 17–29.
The paper examines the fear of crime as it relates to
the mental health of the elderly.

66. Pennsylvania Commission on Crime and Delinquency.
'Strategies to Reduce the Impact of Crime that
Victimizes the Elderly in Pennsylvania,' (in)
J.J. Costa ed. *Abuse of the Elderly*, 1984, 41–56.
A summary of a research project to examine the problem
of crime that victimizes the elderly in Pennsylvania.

67. Powell, D.E. 'The Crimes Against the Elderly,' *Journal
of Gerontological Social Work*, 3(Fall 1980), 27–39.
An average survey of crimes committed in a metropolitan
area will not support the general belief that most
older persons suffer serious problems due to crime.
This is because most serious crimes against the elderly
are not reported. It seems survey data support the
theory that more older women than older men fall victims of crime.

68. Solicitor General of Canada. *Crimes Against the
Elderly*: Bibliography, Ottawa: 1985.
A Canadian bibliography 1985–1986 of items related to
crime against the elderly.

69. Solicitor General of Canada. 'Criminal Victimization of
Elderly Canadians.' Bulletin #6, 1985.
A statistical analysis of a criminal victimization
survey of Canadian elderly.

70. Solicitor General of Canada. Crimes Against the
    Elderly. Ottawa: 1985.
    A folder containing varied items including articles and
    statistics related to crimes against the elderly.

71. Viano, E.C. 'Victimology: An Overview.' (in) J. Kosberg
    ed. *Abuse and Maltreatment of the Elderly*, 1983. 1-18.
    The victim is an integral part of the crime situation.
    One needs to bring the victim's plight to the attention
    of the community.

Definitions of abuse

72. Health and Welfare Canada. Abuse and Neglect of the
    Elderly. Ottawa. National Clearinghouse on Family
    Violence, 1986.
    Some basic facts and definitions about elderly abuse in
    Canada.

73. Johnson, T. 'Critical Issues in the Definition of Elder
    Mistreatment.' (in) K.A. Pillemer and R.S. Wolf, eds.
    Elder Abuse: Conflict in the Family, 1986, 167-196.
    A critical analysis of existing research and
    definitions related to elder abuse.

74. Phillips, L. 'Elder Abuse-What is it? Who Says So?'
    Geriatric Nursing 4(May-June 1983) 167-70.
    Discusses problems related to defining elder abuse and
    describing the characteristics of abusive or neglectful
    relationships. In an investigation of abuse among 74
    frail elderly, nurses were asked to identify abused
    elders through the use of a particular definition of
    abuse and abusive situations. The identification of
    abuse was affected by the observer's personal back-
    ground and sympathies, by respect for the elder's
    right to self-determination, by long-established pat-
    terns of family interaction, and by characteristics
    and behavior of the elder and the caregiver.

75. Podnieks, E. 'Abuse of the Elderly: When Caregivers
    Cease to Care,' *Perspectives*, 9(Winter 1985), 10-12.
    A concise summary of definition, categories, incidence,
    identification and intervention in the problem of elder
    abuse.

Education and training materials

76. Costa, J.J. 'Education and Training Materials: Films, Booklets and Pamphlets, Educational Programs.' (in) J.J. Costa ed. *Abuse of the Elderly*, 1984, 161-74. Addresses to obtain various visual aids and printed material are noted in this chapter of the book.

77. Galbraith, M., Zdorkowski, W. and R. Todd, 'Teaching the Investigation of Elder Abuse,' *Journal of Gerontological Nursing*, 10(December 1984) 21-5. Describes teaching and research tools available to aid nursing leaders in schools, hospitals, and other facilities in educating students and other health care workers about elder abuse. Practitioners and policy makers are becoming increasingly aware of elder abuse, but the research in this area is somewhat circumscribed. Elder abuse surveys frequently suffer from methodological, definitional, and categorical limitations, although their similar findings suggest a broadly accurate image of elder abuse.

Ethnicity and abuse

78. Cazenave, N.A. 'Elder Abuse and Black Americans: Incidence, Correlates, Treatment, and Prevention.' (in) J. Kolsberg ed. *Abuse and Maltreatment of the Elderly*, 1983, 187-203. A sociologist discusses how elder abuse is affected by age and race with emphasis on the Black population in the U.S.A.

79. Nerenberg,L. ed. *Elder Abuse in the Asian Community*. San Francisco: Consortium for Elder Abuse Prevention, 1986. A summary of proceedings of a conference on the problems of elder abuse of Asians.

Familial abuse: domestic abuse

80. Douglas, R.L. 'Domestic Neglect and Abuse of the Elderly: Implications for Research and Service,' *Family Relations*, 32(July 1983), 395-402. Until 1978 no information was published about domestic mistreatment of the elderly in their homes by relatives

or other domestic caregivers. Between 1978 and 1980 six separate investigations of neglect and abuse of elderly persons in their homes were conducted in the United States. Of these studies two were observational case studies, one was a review of medical records, two were mail surveys of human service providers and one was a field study with personal interviews with community practitioners and professionals. All of these investigations agree that a substantial but undocumented problem of domestic neglect and abuse of the elderly exists. The variety and severity of mistreatment ranges from reasonably benign to very severe, and causal theories are numerous. This paper reviews the existing and very limited state of knowledge in this new area of concern, and highlights the findings of the Michigan field study with emphasis on a comparative analysis of findings among different kinds of community professionals and practitioners.

81. Halamandaris, V.J. 'Fraud and Abuse in Nursing Homes.' (in) J. Kosberg ed. *Abuse and Maltreatment of the Elderly*, 1983, 104-14.
A senior lawyer documents widespread fraud and abuse among nursing homes participating in the Medicaid program.

82. Harbin, T. and J. Madden, 'Battered Parents: A New Syndrome,' *American Journal of Psychiatry*. 136(October 1979) 1288-91.
The authors identify a new syndrome of family violence: parent battering. Relevant dynamics include individual characteristics of the parent batterer, distortions in the generational authority hierarchy, the role of secrets and denial, and cultural influences. The authors conclude, on the basis of their clinical work with these families, that this subtype of family violence is distinct from child and spouse abuse.

83. Hickey, T. and R.L. Douglass, 'Mistreatment of the Elderly in the Domestic Setting: An Exploratory Study,' *American Journal of Public Health*. 71(May 1981) 500-7.
Professionals and practitioners (No. 228) involved in providing services to the elderly were interviewed regarding their experiences with the mistreatment of

older people by their families. Semi-structured questions dealt with: case identification and follow-up procedures; perceptions of etiological factors; and descriptive typologies from illustrative case histories. Findings indicated that domestic mistreatment of the elderly was familiar to most professionals interviewed, to the extent that 60 per cent of the respondents dealt with such cases on a weekly basis.

84. Jacobs, M. 'More Than a Million Older Americans Abused Physically and Mentally Each Year,' *Perspective on Aging*, 13(December 1984) 19–20.
Elder abuse is a growing problem that is receiving increased public attention. Domestic abuse of the elderly may be physical, psychological, material, neglect, or a violation of rights. The typical victim is a 75-year-old white, middle-class widow. The abusers are relatives in 84 per cent of the cases, and 75 per cent of victims live with the abusers.

85. Kosberg, J.I. 'The Special Vulnerability of Elderly Parents.' (in) J. Kosberg ed. *Abuse and Maltreatment of the Elderly*, 1983, 263–75.
A discussion of the abuse or maltreatment of the elderly by their families.

86. Pillemer, K. 'The Dangers of Dependency: New Findings on Domestic Violence Against the Elderly,' *Social Problems*, 33(December 1985) 146–85.
Drawing on data from a case-control study of physical abuse of the elderly, the author examines conflicting hypotheses regarding the degree of mutual dependency of the abuser and the abused. On the basis of quantitative and qualitative analyses, the elderly victims were more likely to be supporting the dependent abuser, materially and/or emotionally.

87. Steinmetz, S. 'Battered Parents,' *Society*. 15(July/Aug. 1978) 54–5.
This article describes how, under the present economic structure of our capitalist system, the role of the elderly is limited to consumption rather than production, and that therefore the elderly are 'valued' less in our society. It is felt that this negative societal view of the elderly can ultimately contribute to elder

abuse and/or neglect through our selective inattention to the needs and requirements of the elderly population.

Family violence

88. Brown, J.A. 'Combatting the Roots of Family Violence,' *Journal of Social Welfare* 6, No. 2. (1979–1980) 17–24. Similar dynamics heavily influenced by role expectations can be found in acts of abuse, whether the victim is a child, a wife, or an elderly parent. Abused persons find themselves in positions characterized by dependence and helplessness. The act of violence is put into operation by stress that threatens the role image of the dominant person involved. However, no one reason accounts for violent acts in the family. Just as the reporting of child abuse has become mandatory, any act of violence within the family requires reporting. Currently this is not the case in the areas of spouse abuse of abuse to the elderly. This attitude sanctions and perpetuates future acts of violence within the family. Until society recognizes its role in creating violence in the family and its responsibility in curtailing it, such acts will continue, and the family will continue its role in educating and nurturing successive generations of potential abusers.

89. Canadian Association of Social Work Administrators in Health Facilities. *Domestic Violence Protocol Manual: For Social Workers in Health Facilities*. Ottawa, Ont.: National Clearinghouse of Family Violence, Health and Welfare, Canada, 1985. The phrase domestic violence encompasses all types of abuse that occur in the home: physical and sexual abuse of children and adults, and abuse or neglect of elderly persons. Since victims of these types of abuse often turn to health care facilities for treatment, their contact with the social worker in these settings may be their first genuine opportunity to discuss their experiences. Sensitive interviewing skills are crucial to creating the trust necessary for exploring options.

90. Finkelhor, D. 'Common Features of Family Abuse.' (in) *The Dark Side of Families*. ed. by D. Finkelhor et al. Beverly Hills: Sage, 1983, 17–28. Some of the insights found on examining the commonalities and differences among forms of violence and abuse.

91. Gelles, R.J. and C.P. Cornell. *Intimate Violence in Families*. Beverly Hills, Ca.: Sage Publications 1985.
To understand family violence, we must first understand the operation and function of the entire family system. This is the premise of the authors' overview of family violence. They contend that one form of violence in the home may be connected to other forms. Thus, the examination covers child abuse, courtship violence, spouse abuse, sibling violence, adolescent maltreatment, parent abuse, and elder abuse. They focus on physical violence.

92. Lecours, W. and J. Roy. 'Violence and the Marginalization of the Elderly in Today's Society,' *Canada's Mental Health*, 30(September 1982), 25-7; 35.
This paper discusses the place violence holds in the lives of the elderly in the province of Quebec.

93. Star, B. 'Patterns in Family Violence,' *Social Casework*, 61(June 1980) 339-46.
The prevalence of physical and sexual abuse among family members is greater than most people realize. A generic approach to the study of abuse in families suggests that there are many similarities among assaulter characteristics, victim characteristics, and the family interactions that underlie all forms of family violence.

94. Straus, M.A., Gelles, R.J. and S. Steinmetz. *Behind Closed Doors: Violence in the American Family*. New York: Anchor Press, Doubleday, 1980.
Based on 2000 interviews it shows how domestic violence cuts across all socio-economic levels of society.

Films

95. Solicitor General of Canada. Crimes Against the Elderly: Films. Ottawa, 1985.
A list of 14 films related to crimes against the elderly.

Fraud and the elderly

96. Beck, L.M. and L.R. Phillips. 'The Unseen Abuse: Why Financial Maltreatment of the Elderly Goes Unrecognized,' *Journal of Gerontological Nursing*, Vol. 10, (December 1984) 26-30.

An interview with two elder abuse authorities on the problem of financial extortion and exploitation of the elderly by relatives, friends and caregivers. Identification is blocked by dependency, lack of access to protection and lack of alternatives, along with the fear of retaliation.

97. McGhee, J.L. 'The Vulnerability of Elderly Consumers,' *International Journal of Aging and Human Development* 17, No 3 (1983) 223–46.
Research interest in the vulnerability of the elderly to consumer fraud has increased in recent years. Consumer surveys & studies of complaint data permit the examination of hypothesized indicators of vulnerability for samples of older & younger consumers. A review of the research shows that patterns of consumption, situational characteristics, education & product knowledge, awareness of deception, psychological losses, social isolation, & psychosocial transitions influence the elderly's vulnerability & ability to cope with consumer abuse.

98. Pepper, C.D. 'Frauds Against the Elderly.' (in) J. Kosberg ed. *Abuse and Maltreatment of the Elderly*, 1983, 68–83.
A senior congressman points out that senior citizens constitute 11 per cent of the American population but are almost 30 per cent of the victims of crime. He discusses the types of frauds which the elderly experience.

99. Stathopoulos, P.A. 'Consumer Advocacy and Abuse of Elders in Nursing Homes.' (in) J. Kosberg ed. *Abuse and Maltreatment of the Elderly*, 1983, 335–54.
A social work professor discusses the activities and strategies of a consumer advocacy organization in Massachusetts to deal with elder abuse in nursing homes.

Historical views

100. Reinharz, S. 'Loving and Hating One's Elders: Twin Themes in Legend and Literature,' (in) K.A. Pillemer and R.S. Wolf eds. *Elder Abuse; Conflict in the Family*, 1986, 25–48.

The socio-psychological bond between adults and children in historical perspective is discussed.

101. Stearns, P.J. 'Old Age Family Conflict: The Perspective of the past.' (in) K.A. Pillemer and R.S. Wolf eds., *Elder Abuse: Conflict in the Family*, 1986, 3-24.
An historical analysis of intergenerational conflict in Western history.

Identification

102. O'Malley, T., Everitt, D., O'Malley, H., and E. Campion, 'Identifying and Preventing Family-Mediated Abuse and Neglect of Elderly Persons,' *Annals of Internal Medicine*. 98(June 1983), 998-1005.
This article presents an outline in order to aid physicians in the identification, assessment, management, follow-up, and prevention of elder abuse and neglect. Theories of causation, definitional problems encountered, and possible intervention strategies are discussed.

103. O'Malley, T. 'Identifying and Preventing Family-Mediated Abuse and Neglect,' *Caring* 5(Jan. 1986), 28-30.
Outlines the problem of abuse and neglect of the elderly, discusses a philosophy of intervention and considers related ethical issues. Discusses the definition of elder abuse and presents background information on its frequency and victims. Shows that abuse and neglect are parts of a long term pattern of family interaction and that conclusions drawn from brief interviews may not be valid. Suggests that intervention is more readily accepted if attention is focussed on the care needs of the elderly person, and also recommends a multidisciplinary team approach. Stresses that intervention in cases of elder abuse should be negotiated with the elderly and the family, not imposed as in cases of child abuse, and should aim at the least restrictive alternative. Summarizes theories that have been advanced on elder abuse, and enumerates marker conditions signal potential cases of abuse and neglect. Recommends an intervention approach based on observing the extent of the care needs of the elderly person and the caretaking role of the abuser.

Concludes that home care providers must lobby for more legislation to enhance the health and welfare of the elderly.

104. Phillips, L.R. and J.F. Rempusheski. 'Making Decisions about Elder Abuse,' *Social Casework* 67(March 1986), 131–40.
Case detection of elder abuse is limited by denial, lack of procedures and intervention options. This study deals with the relationship between definition and detection, and the relationship between detection and intervention. Cultural and personal norms, moral perceptions of the abuser and accountability and self-protection all affected definition, detection and intervention.

105. Rathbone–McCuan, E. and B. Voyles, 'Case Detection of Abused Elderly Parents,' *American Journal of Psychiatry* 139(Feb. 1982) 189–92.
At this early stage of research, intrafamily violence affecting elderly members is difficult to detect or assess, because it encompasses a wide variety of behaviours ranging from self–abuse to life endangering actions by others. To prevent cases of geriatric abuse, two major barriers must be overcome: denial by professionals that the problem exists and lack of procedures for case detection. Physical indicators of possible elder abuse include bruises and welts on the chest, shoulders, back, arms or legs; cigarette burns, rope or chain burns from confinement, and burns caused by some object, lacerations and abrasions on the lips, eyes or other parts of the face, and head injuries such as absence of hair or hemorrhage beneath the scalp. Cases of abuse have been detected in which the elderly person was ill but remained in the home without proper medical attention and was offered no care by the child. Case detection requires training and education.

106. Sengstock, M.C., M. Hwalek. 'A Critical Analysis of Measures for the Identification of Physical Abuse and Neglect of the Elderly,' *Home Health Care Service Quarterly* 6(1985/86), 27–39.
An analysis and critique of seven elder abuse identification indices focused on areas of Physical

Abuse and Physical Neglect. Recommendations for
improved methods include specificity, differential
diagnosis and sexual abuse identification.

Incidence

107. Champlin, L. 'The Battered Elderly,' *Geriatrics*.
37(July 1982) 115-21.
This article briefly reviews the extent of the elder
abuse problem in the United States, and then examines
why attempts to intervene in such cases are frustrated.
Legal, medical, and social restraints are seen as
barriers preventing social welfare officials from
assisting the abused elderly.

108. Floyd, J. 'Collecting Data on Abuse of the Elderly,'
Journal of Gerontological Nursing, 10(December 1984)
11-15.
Explores the need for documenting the incidence of
elder abuse. To examine abuse of the elderly it is
necessary to define the term; to research and document
the existence of abuse; to determine the kinds of
information health and legal professionals require to
assess cases of abuse; and to understand the barriers
to case reporting. To serve elders who appear in need
of help, nurses must deepen their awareness regarding
abuse; make thorough assessments; gain the confidence
of their elderly clients; and assist families through
interviews, counseling, and referrals.

109. Long, C. 'Geriatric Abuse,' *Issues in Mental Health
Nursing*. 3(1981), 123-35.
The problems of documenting the incidence of abuse are
discussed, followed by a detailed case study of a
potentially abusive situation. Possible solutions to
the problem are proposed.

110. Poertner, J. 'Estimating the Incidence of Abused Older
Persons,' *Journal of Gerontological Social Work*
9(Spring 1986) 3-15.
Report of a statewide study on abuse in Illinois
utilizing a stratified random sample of communities,
in which service providers were surveyed. From this
sample, statewide incidence rates were developed.

111. Ross, M., P.A. Ross and M.C. Ross, 'Abuse of the
     Elderly,' *Canadian Nurse* 81(February 1985), 36-9.
     A review of trends contributing to elder abuse and
     studies of incidence. Guides for nurses in identifi-
     cation and intervention in elder abuse cases are pre-
     sented. A one-page questionnaire for data collection is
     included.

Institutional abuse

112. Reece, D., Waltz, T., and H. Hageboeck. 'Intergenera-
     tional Care providers of Non-Institutionalized Frail
     Elderly: Characteristics and Consequences,' *Journal of
     Gerontological Social Work* 5, No. 3(1983) pp. 21-34.
     Presented is a report on the care provided to forty-one
     institutionalized frail older people by their children
     or grandchildren. The study explored three aspects of
     intergenerational family caregiving: the characteris-
     tics of the offspring caregivers, their perceptions of
     both the positive and negative impacts of providing
     care, and their perceptions of supplementary assistance
     needed and desired from outside agencies in carrying
     out the caregiving tasks. The sample of caregivers
     shared many common characteristics. Most of them came
     from relatively stable and cohesive family constella-
     tions. Few were divorced. Most respondents indicated a
     close and long-term relationship with the older person.
     Fulfilling the role of a primary caregiver was not
     necessarily a burden to be endured.

113. Tarbox, A.R. 'The Elderly in Nursing Homes: Psycho-
     logical Aspects of Neglect,' *Clinical Gerontologist* 1,
     (Summer 1983) pp. 39-52.
     Psychological abuse and neglect, particularly in their
     less obvious forms, may be the most frequent types of
     elder abuse in nursing homes. Forms of psychological
     abuse or neglect are lack of cleanliness and attrac-
     tiveness in the physical environment, inadequate diet,
     lack of attention by staff to grooming of patients,
     infantilization, and benign neglect. Environmental
     deprivation created by the lack of human contact or a
     physically stimulus-poor environment can lead to re-
     gression, dependency, and helplessness.

114. Urban, A.J. 'Nursing Home Patient Abuse Reporting: An

Analysis of the Washington Statutory Response,' *Gonzaga Law Review* 16, No. 3(1981) 609–35.
An examination of the metamorphosis of nursing home regulations in Washington over the past 30 years precedes discussion of the state's Patient Abuse Reporting System (PARS). An effective PARS requires that it be well publicized, have a quick response time to complaints, provide feedback to the complainant as to the results and proposed corrective action, and have strong penalties. The Washington PARS, in its present form, has some but not all of these prerequisites.

Intervention

115. Astrein, B., Steinberg, A. and J. Duhl. 'Working With Abused Elders: Assessment, Advocacy, and Intervention.' Worcester, MA: University Center on Aging, University of Massachusetts Medical Center, 1984.
Advice is provided to practitioners for dealing with situations involving elders in a domestic setting who are the victims of abuse or neglect by relatives or other informal caregivers. The issues and principles discussed are based on the findings of three model projects for treating elder abuse and neglect in Massachusetts, Rhode Island, and Syracuse, NY. Profiles of the abused and the abusers are presented. The prevalence of different types of abuse is examined, and theories of elder abuse are reviewed. A case level approach to intervention is outlined that includes reporting, investigation, assessment, service planning, and service delivery. The major features of the three model projects are described. Case examples are used to illustrate the client pathway followed by each project, and the pros and cons of each project are analyzed. It is concluded that since the problem of elder abuse generally is rooted in family dynamics, it must be treated by addressing the needs of the entire family. A comprehensive and well-coordinated response is required for effective intervention. The four appendixes contain diagrams of sample client pathways, an instrument for assessment of abuse or neglect, a resource list, and an annotated bibliography.

116. Kinderknecht, C.H. 'In Home Social Work With Abused or Neglected Elderly: An Experimental Guide to Assessment

and Treatment,' *Journal of Gerontological Social Work*, 9(Spring 1986) 29-42.
A guide to assessment and intervention of elder abuse among home-care clients. Includes indications, strategies and limitations on professional intervention and investigation.

117. Phillips, L.R. and V.F. Rempusheski. 'A Decision-Making Model for Diagnosing and Intervening in Elder Abuse and Neglect,' *Nursing Research* 34(May-June 1985), 134-9.
A four-stage decision-making model, based on grounded theory is presented. Tape-recorded interviews with twenty-nine health-care providers supplied data. Model describes pathways from decision-making to intervention.

118. Pillemer, K. 'Domestic Violence Against the Elderly.' Durham: University of New Hampshire, Family Research Laboratory, October 1985.
A working paper which discusses the major data sources available on elder abuse and strategies for intervention. To be published as a chapter in a forthcoming book.

119. Potter, J.F. and A. Jameton. 'Respecting the Choices of Neglected Elders: Autonomy or Abuse.' (in) M.W. Galbraith ed. *Convergence in Aging*, 1986, 95-109.
A discussion of intervention in elder abuse, including case examples.

Justice system: legal aspects

120. Ambrogi, D. and C. London. 'Elder Abuse Laws,' *Generations*, 10(Fall 1985) 37-9.
A brief description of the types of stresses and social configurations which can contribute to abuse are presented. It is emphasized that mandatory reporting laws must be accompanied by a range of supportive ameliorative and corrective services.

121. American Public Welfare Association. Executive Summary: A Comprehensive Analysis of State Policy and Practice Related to Elder Abuse. Report #2: A Focus on State Reporting Systems. Washington, D.C., Sept. 1986.
This report presents the results of a review of the elder abuse reporting system forms, instructions and

procedures currently used by states in managing elder
abuse information. The review was conducted jointly by
the American Public Welfare Association (APWA) and the
National Association of State Units on Aging (NASUA)
between April and July 1986. State social service and
aging agencies were asked to submit copies of the
forms, the instructions for using them, procedures
followed in elder abuse cases, and statistical reports
produced by their elder abuse reporting systems.

In response to this request, more than 200 data collection forms were received from 41 states. Part 1 of
this report presents an analysis of the data items collected by all of the respondents and identifies where
in the state/local system the data may be found. Part 2
contains a narrative description of the operation of
the elder abuse reporting systems in five states.

122. David, M.A. 'An Ombudsman's Perspective.' (in) M.W.
Galbraith ed. *Convergence in Aging*, 1986, 125–38.
This chapter explains the role of the ombudsman who
deals with issues of elder abuse, neglect and exploitation in Kansas.

123. Faulkner, L.R. 'Mandating the Reporting of Suspected
Cases of Elder Abuse: An Inappropriate, Ineffective and
Ageist Response to the Abuse of Older Adults,' *Family
Law Quarterly*. 16(Spring 1982), 69–91.
This articles examines the issue of mandatory reporting
for elder abuse cases in order to assist policy-makers
in the area. Effectiveness of transferring mandatory
reporting techniques used in cases of suspected child
abuse to cases of elder abuse is discussed and
questioned.

124. Guinn, M.J. 'Elder Abuse and Neglect Raise New
Dilemmas,' *Generations* 10 No. 2(1985) 22–5.
The ethical and legal dilemmas of practitioners faced
with elder abuse are discussed. Basic constitutional
rights may at times conflict with protection needs for
vulnerable elderly who are abused and neglected. Rights
of the older adults, the caregivers and practitioners
should be recognized and discussed.

125. Katz, K.D. 'Elder Abuse,' *Journal of Family Law*. 18(4),
(1979–1980) 659–722.

The author discusses some of the legal problems surrounding the legislation of mandatory reporting for
cases of elder abuse. Comparisons are made with current
child abuse reporting statutes, and it is suggested
that a more effective response would be the establishment of voluntary prevention and treatment services.

126. Mancini, M. 'Adult Abuse Laws,' *American Journal of
Nursing*, (April 1980), 739-40.
Twelve states have enacted comprehensive adult protection laws to ensure that people who are aged, infirm,
or incapable of self-care receive essential life-
sustaining services. This article is an attempt to
provide community health nurses with an understanding
of how these laws operate.

127. Nathanson, P. 'An Overview of Legal Issues, Services,
and Resources.' (in) J. Kosberg ed. *Abuse and Maltreatment of the Elderly*, 1983, 303-15.
A law professor reviews legal services and neighbour-
hood dispute resolution related to elder abuse. The
legal problems facing the elderly are also discussed.

128. Oaker, M.R. and C.A. Miller. 'Federal Legislation to
Protect the Elderly.' (in) J. Kosberg ed. *Abuse and
Maltreatment of the Elderly*, 1983, 422-35.
Reviews the federal legislation in protecting older
Americans from abuse.

129. Salend, E., Kane, R.A., Satz, M. and J. Pynoos. 'Elder
Abuse Reporting: Limitations of Statutes,' *The
Gerontologist*, 24(February 1984), 61-7.
This study compares 16 state elder abuse reporting
statutes and analyzes their implementation. Generally,
the statutes have failed to ensure consistent information about elder abuse within or across states. Although statistical summaries generated by the laws are
meagre, neglect is more often reported than abuse and,
within the neglect category, self-neglect predominates;
little prosecutory activity was noted. Definitions were
imprecise and varied from statute to statute. Suggestions for improving reporting policies are made.

130. Sengstock, M.C. and M. Hwalek. 'Domestic Abuse of the
Elderly: Which Cases Involve the Police?' *Journal of*

Interpersonal Violence Vol. 1, (September 1986), 335-49.
Because the elder victim is an adult, but often in a highly dependent position to abuser, elder abuse has common elements with both spouse abuse and child abuse. In this analysis of police involvement in 77 elder abuse cases from a 1981 study and a random sample of 1983 cases from the adult protective services files were reviewed. Police were found to be rarely involved even when clear violations of law occurred, due to reluctance, perceived difficulties and time involved.

131. Sloan, I.J., (Ed.) *Law and Legislation of Elderly Abuse*. Dobbs Ferry, N.Y.: Oceana Publications, 1983.
Reviews and synthesizes existing information on the law and legislation related to abuse of the elderly. Introductory chapters review research studies on the nature and causes of elder abuse. A 1980 survey by the Senate Special Committee on Aging identified 25 states that have some type of adult protective services legislation. The provisions and coverage of these laws vary widely in scope, as do the provisions of the laws that require reporting on and investigation of suspected cases of abuse. Sixteen states have reporting legislation, the majority of which was passed within the last 5 years. The lack of uniform definitions, standards, and procedures is a common problem of reporting legislation as a whole.

132. Thobaben, M. and L. Anderson. 'Reporting Elder Abuse – It's the Law,' *American Journal of Nursing*, 85, (April 1985), 371-4.
A summary in chart form of the laws of the fifty states, what each state considers abuse, who must report it and the penalties for failure to report.

133. Traxler, A.J. 'Elder Abuse Laws: A Survey of State Statutes.' (in) M.W. Galbraith ed. *Convergence in Aging*, 1986, 139-67.
A psychologist reviews the content of 50 states and the District of Columbia's elder abuse laws or proposed legislation.

134. Walker, J.C. 'Protective Services for the Elderly: Connecticut's Experience.' (in) J. Kosberg ed.

Abuse and Maltreatment of the Elderly, 1983, 292–302.
The State Ombudsman describes the legislation passed in
Connecticut, related to the elderly, including the
Ombudsman's office.

Newsletters

135. Family-Violence Bulletin-*Quarterly*. Tyler, Texas:
     Psychology Department, University of Texas, 1987.
     A quarterly bulletin which lists resources in family
     violence, including elder abuse.

136. Health and Welfare. Elder Abuse in Canada. *Vis à Vis*,
     1(Autumn 1983).
     A special issue of a newsletter published by the
     National Clearinghouse on Family Violence.

137. University of Massachusetts Medical Center. *Elder Abuse
     Report*. Worcester, Mass.: University Center on Aging,
     1986.
     This newsletter is produced four times per year. It
     includes research notes, new publication notes, and
     other information related to elder abuse ($10 per
     annum).

Overview

138. Callahan, J.J. 'Elder Abuse Programming: Will it Help
     the Elderly?' *The Urban and Social Change Review*. 15
     (Summer 1982), 15–16.
     The author questions the effectiveness of conceptual-
     izing elder abuse as a separate and distinct behaviour
     for which specialized programming is required. Defini-
     tional problems are discussed, as are problems of dif-
     ferential reporting and of 'agenda setting.' It is
     suggested that elder abuse should be seen more as a
     side issue, and not as the centre of social policy.

139. Fox, R. 'The Multiple Faces of Elder Abuse,' *Geriatric
     Medicine* (Canada), 1(April 1985), 105–11.
     The author includes collective societal abuse of the
     elderly as a group as well as the categories of
     individual abuse. The latter includes physical and
     psychological mistreatment and neglect. Predisposing

factors are described and incidence reported, along with recommendations for future societal response.

140. Galbraith, M.W. 'Elder Abuse: An Overview.' (in) M.W. Galbraith ed. *Convergence in Aging*, 1986, 5-27.
A comprehensive summary of existing information on elder abuse.

141. Ghent, W.R., Da Silva, N.P. and M.E. Farren. 'Family Violence: Guidelines for Recognition and Management,' *Canadian Medical Association Journal* 132(March 1, 1985), 541-53.
Elder abuse is one section (547-548) of this article. Incidence figures, abuse categories, diagnostic cues and a guide for assessment and management are given. A list of Canadian Family Violence service and information resources are given, arranged by province.

142. Goldstein, S. and A. Blank, 'The Elderly: Abused or Abusers?' *Canadian Medical Association Journal*. 127 (September 15, 1982), 455-6.
This editorial addresses the concern of viewing abuse of the elderly in a biased and oversimplistic way. Discussed are the many factors involved in the care of the elderly and how increased demands and limited emotional resources of caregivers can easily lead to an abusive situation. Also mentioned are the special problems involved in the care of elderly persons who are confused.

143. Hudson, J.E. *Elder Abuse: An Overview*. Toronto: Programme in Gerontology, University of Toronto, Research Paper No. 7, 1986.
A review of literature on elder abuse up to 1985.

144. Kimsey, L.R., Tarbox, A.R. and D.F. Bragg. 'Abuse of the Elderly - The Hidden Agenda 1. The Caretakers and the Categories of Abuse,' *American Geriatrics Society Journal*, 29(October 1981), 465-72.
An overview of the abuse of the elderly is presented in an effort to guide future research. It identifies categories of caretakers for the aged as formal (institutional settings) and informal (family, neighbours, sitters). Information is presented from a task force

report on the status of nursing homes in Texas. Physical, psychological, material, and fiscal categories of abuse are delineated. Findings of the report revealed that deliberate physical abuse by formal caretakers was the least common; physical neglect was far more frequent. Psychological abuse occurred most often in the area of benign neglect. Material abuse included theft, chiefly of personal items. Fiscal abuse centered around embezzling patients' trust funds, overcharging for services, failing to notify the state of the death or departure of a patient, abusing medication, and artificially upgrading Medicaid recipients' classifications. Possible causes of abuse are reviewed.

145. Lattanzio, G. 'Elder Abuse,' *Ontario Association of Professional Social Workers Metronews*, January 1987, 20-2.
A short summary of elder abuse.

146. Lee, R.L. and R. Trotta. 'Abused Parents: A Hidden Family Problem,' *Journal of Family Violence*. 1(March 1986), 99-110.
The purpose of this paper is to explore the following: characteristics of elderly victims and their perpetrators, frequency of the act, factors that may cause abuse, intervention strategies, and policy concern that impact on this life-threatening behaviour. Suggestions for future work in this area are offered.

147. Pedrick-Cornell, C. and R. Gelles. 'Elder Abuse: The Status of Current Knowledge,' *Family Relations*. 31(July 1982), 457-65.
This paper examines the current state of knowledge of elder abuse and examines the limitations of current research on the extent, patterns, and causes of such mistreatment. Suggestions are offered to researchers and practitioners in terms of intervention and prevention.

148. Pierce, R.L. and R. Trotta. 'Abused Parents: A Hidden Family Problem,' *Journal of Family Violence*, 1(March 1986), 99-110.
Characteristics of elderly victims and their abusers, frequency of the act, factors that may cause abuse, intervention strategies, and policy concerns are explored.

149. Podnieks, E. 'Elder Abuse: It's Time We Did Something About It,' *The Canadian Nurse*, 81(December 1985), 36-9.
A good overview of the problem of elder abuse in Canada.

150. Schlesinger, B. 'Elderly Abuse: The Fourth Horseman,' *Journal*(OACAS) 29(May 1985), 13-16.
A short introduction to the topic of elder abuse.

151. Westbrook, G.J. 'Perspectives on Aging - Elder Abuse and Neglect,' *Continuing Care Coordinator* 4(January 1986), 48-9.
Reviews the types of elder abuse, its causes, settings, incidence, and intervention strategies. The abuse may be physical, psychological, material/financial, or a violation of legal rights. Most overt abuse occurs in the homes of relatives, while neglect is most prevalent in extended care homes. It is estimated that about 20 per cent of the aged are victims of abuse or neglect; most of the victims are over 75, female, and have at least one chronic medical problem and/or cognitive impairment. A variety of factors contribute to elder abuse, including alcohol or substance abuse, inappropriate caregivers, financial problems or unemployment of the abuser, irritating characteristics of the victim, and stress and frustration resulting from the caregiving burden. Interventions include education of professional and paraprofessional caregivers about the problem, as well as education of family caregivers about caring for their relative and about the community services available to them.

Physical abuse

152. Anderson, C.L. 'Abuse and Neglect Among the Elderly,' *Journal of Gerontological Nursing*. 7(February 1981), 77-85.
Several case histories are used to illustrate various situations in which physical abuse and neglect are directed toward the elderly by informal caregivers. Society, families, and health professionals are seen as perpetuating the abuse. The negative attitudes held by society toward the elderly are also examined in this context.

153. Bahr, R.T. 'The Battered Elderly: Physical and
     Psychological Abuse,' *Family and Community Health*,
     4(August 1981), 61-9.
     Abuse of the elderly can be either physical or psycho-
     logical, and can be inflicted by youths roaming the
     streets or breaking into the homes of older persons, by
     adult children of elderly parents, and by personnel in
     long-term care facilities. A major problem regarding
     abuse cases is the reluctance of the elderly to report
     such action, especially out of fear of retaliation by
     family members or nursing home staff who could withhold
     essential services. Health care professionals need to
     be more accessible to the elderly and to advocate on
     their behalf. Specific actions that can be taken in-
     clude launching education programs for the general
     public on the aging process, the elderly, and the
     causes of their behaviour; identifying families in
     which abusive actions may occur and referring them
     to agencies that can aid in lessening family stress;
     and reporting any evidence of abuse to appropriate
     agencies for action. This article overviews the rele-
     vant literature and discusses various definitions of
     assault, battery, and physical and psychological abuse.

154. Podnieks, E. 'The Victimization of Older Persons.'
     Psychiatric Nursing, January-March 1987, 6-11.
     A general overview of physical, social and psycho-
     logical aspects related to the victimization of the
     elderly.

Physically disabled and abuse

155. Luppens, J. and E.E. Lau. 'The Mentally and Physically
     Impaired Elderly Relative: Consequences for Family
     Care.' (in) J. Kosberg ed. *Abuse and Maltreatment of
     the Elderly*, 1983, 204-19.
     A discussion of elderly abuse of the mentally and
     physically impaired population.

156. Stever, J.L. 'Abuse of the Physically Disabled
     Elderly.' (in) J. Kosberg ed. *Abuse and Maltreatment of
     the Elderly*, 1983, 234-50.
     Approximately 14 per cent of elderly community resi-
     dents are restricted in physical mobility. The author
     discusses abuse to this group of senior citizens.

Professionals and elder abuse

157. Bookin, D. and R.E. Dunkle. 'Elder Abuse: Issues for
     the Practicioner,' *Social Casework*, 66(January 1985),
     3-12.
     Workers assigned to cases of elder abuse experience
     significant proglems related not only to the nature of
     the problem but also to their own feelings, biases, and
     attitudes about violence and the aging. This article
     examines the problems and suggests strategies for
     dealing with them.

158. Hickey, T. and R.L. Douglass, 'Neglect and Abuse of
     Older Family Members: Professionals' Perspectives and
     Case Experiences,' *Gerontologist*. 21(April 1981), 171-76.
     This is a data-based framework for understanding domes-
     tic mistreatment of older people by family members.
     Evidence from interviews of 228 professionals suggests
     that environmental contexts and situational problems
     serve as triggers to such behaviour, which is primarily
     based in the flawed development of the perpetrator and
     in disordered family relationships. Recommendations are
     that there is a need for more formal systems of care
     and protective services, as well as an increased need
     for education, training, and research.

159. Matlow, J.R. and J.B. Mayer. 'Elder Abuse: Ethical and
     Practical Dilemmas for Social Work,' *Health and Social
     Work*, 11(Spring 1986), 85-93.
     A description of the role of the social worker in an
     acute care hospital multi-disciplinary team in assess-
     ing elder abuse. Social workers may be caught in an
     ethical conflict in balancing legal requirements, the
     victim's wishes and the reality of resources.

160. O'Brien, J.G., Hudson, M.F., and T.F. Johnson. Health
     Care Provider Survey on Elder Abuse. East Lansing,
     Michigan. 1984. (unpublished)
     3001 health care providers were mailed questionnaires
     to obtain information about intervention of elder abuse
     by doctors and nurses.

161. Palinesar, J. and D.C. Cobb. 'The Physician's Role in
     Detecting and Reporting Elder Abuse,' *The Journal of
     Legal Medicine*. 3(3)1982, 413-41.

This article is an attempt to inform the physician about the basic problem of elder abuse and as well to describe the role of the physician in a formal legal response to the problem. The first section of the paper deals with a basic descriptive analysis of elder abuse, while the second section covers issues of physician liability and of the use of medical expert opinion in cases of elder abuse.

162. Podnieks, E. 'Abuse of the Elderly,' *Canadian Nurse*. 79(May 1983), 34-5.
This paper presents a challenge to health care professionals to examine their own feelings and attitudes towards the elderly. The role of stereotyping and the ways in which attitudes are formed and passed on are discussed. Proposed strategies for prevention are reviewed.

163. Reynolds, E. and S. Stanton. 'Elder Abuse in a Hospital.' (in) J. Kosberg ed. *Abuse and Maltreatment of the Elderly*, 1983, 391-403.
A discussion of the role of nurses in the recognition and reporting of elder abuse.

164. Simson, S., Wilson, L.B., Hermalin, J., and R. Hess, eds. *Aging and Prevention: New Approaches For Preventing Health and Mental Health Problems in Older Adults*, New York: Haworth Press, 1983.
Reviews the state of knowledge of domestic neglect and abuse of the elderly, relating this new information to opportunities that exist for prevention, and focusing on a Michigan survey of community professionals. Of 228 respondents, 156 (68 per cent) were knowledgeable about specific cases of neglect or abuse. Passive neglect was most frequently cited, 150 (66 per cent) reporting knowledge of this form of mistreatment. Relative prevalence, according to most authors, suggests that neglect and emotional types of abuse are considerably more widespread than physical abuse.

165. Solomon, K. 'Victimization by Health Professionals and the Psychologic Response of the Elderly.' (in) J. Kosberg ed. *Abuse and Maltreatment of the Elderly*, 1983, 150-70.

Many elderly are not receiving adequate services in
general and few are receiving adequate mental health
services. Many professionals do not have training in
identifying or assessing emotional problems of the
elderly.

166. Solomon, K. 'Intervention for the Victimized Elderly
     and Sensitization of Health Professionals: Therapeutic
     and Educational Efforts.' (in) J. Kosberg ed. *Abuse and
     Maltreatment of the Elderly*, 1983, 404-21.
     The author examines intervention related to pharmaco-
     logic and nonpharmacologic aspects.

167. Steuer, J. and E. Austin. 'Family Abuse of the
     Elderly,' *Journal of the American Geriatrics Society.*
     28(August 1980), 372-6.
     The purpose of this paper is to sensitize health
     professionals to the phenomenon of elder abuse by
     studying the dynamics of the problem. Characteristics
     of both the abused and of the abusers are documented,
     as are the possible causes of elder mistreatment. Data
     is collected through the examination of 12 cases of
     elder abuse, and various recommendations are made for
     the management of abusive families.

Protective services

168. Bragg, D.F., Kimsey, L.R. and A.R. Tarbox. 'Abuse of
     the Elderly: The Hidden Agenda. II. Future Research and
     Remediation,' *Journal of the American Geriatrics
     Society*, 29(November 1981), 503-7.
     The authors make recommendations for protecting the
     elderly against abuse. Treatment goals for the com-
     munity, medical personnell and the legal profession
     are included.

169. Hooyman, N.R., Rathbone-McCuan, E., and K. Klingbeil.
     'Serving the Vulnerable Elderly: The Detection,
     Intervention, and Prevention of Familial Abuse,' *The
     Urban and Social Change Review*. Vol. 15,(Summer, 1982),
     9-12.
     This article briefly summarizes and critiques the
     empirical knowledge base of elder abuse to date. It
     then addresses some of the barriers encountered when

attempting to develop a comprehensive community response to the problems, and provides the reader with
strategies to help overcome such barriers.

170. Hooyman, N.R. 'Elder Abuse and Neglect: Community
Interventions.; (in) J. Kosberg ed. *Abuse and
Maltreatment of the Elderly*, 1983, 376-90.
A social work professor discusses ways to use existing
community resources and the prevention of elder abuse
and in intervention with abusers and victims.

171. Johnson, D. 'Abuse of the Elderly,' *Nurse Practitioner*.
6(January-February 1981), 29-34.
This article proposes the use of a screening protocol
for identifying cases of elder abuse. A protocol
suggesting subjective and objective data collection,
based on the available literature on abused older
persons as well as on the child abuse model, is
provided as a guideline for nursing professionals.

172. Regan, J.J. 'Protective Services for the Elderly: Benefit or Threat.' (in) J. Kosberg ed. *Abuse and Maltreatment of the Elderly*, 1983, 279-91.
A law professor discusses protective services programs
for the elderly including guardianship.

173. Staudt, M. 'Social Worker As An Advocate in Adult
Protective Services,' *Social Work* 30(May-June 1985),
204-8.
Reviews contemporary adult protective services,
focussing on the potential threats to individuals'
civil rights by involuntary legal interventions. Also
defines the role of social workers in adult protective
services. Provides a brief history of adult protective
services, up to and including the emergence of elder
abuse as a social issue in the later 1970s and 1980s.
Attempts to define the scope of adult protective services.

174. Zborowsky, E. 'Developments in Protective Services: A
Challenge for Social Workers,' *Journal of Gerontological Social Work* 8(Spring-Summer 1985), 71-83.
Reviews the development of protective services for
older people who are vulnerable to abuse, neglect, or
exploitation, and discusses issues remaining to be
resolved. The main forms of protective services for

adults during the first half of the twentieth century
were the states' legal procedures for commitment to a
state mental hospital or for appointment of a guardian.
Interest in protective services for older people
increased dramatically in the 1960s, and seven major
protective research and demonstration projects were
conducted in different parts of the country. Interest
waned again in the 1970s after one of these studies
showed that the demonstration protective service was no
more effective than the usual community control services. Protective services for older people remained
a viable legal and social welfare issue, however, and
concern about the rights of older people in need of
protective services has increased.

Protocols

175. Kerr, R.A. (Coordinator). *Task Force on Family
Violence in Northumberland County: Elder Abuse
Protocol.* Port Hope, Ontario, 1986.
This protocol is written to provide procedures for
human service professionals when dealing with elderly
abuse in Northumberland County. The object of the
protocol is to establish a standardized interdisciplinary approach in the reporting, investigating and
management of elderly abuse.
    The focus is primarily on intrafamilial abuse.

176. Quinn, M.J. and S.T. Tomita. 'Elder Abuse and Neglect:
Written Protocol for Identification and Assessment,'
(in) Quinn and Tomita eds. *Elder Abuse and Neglect.*
New York: Springer Publishing, 1986, 267-74.
A detailed protocol to asses elder abuse.

177. Tomita, S.K. 'Detection and Treatment of Elderly Abuse
and Neglect: A Protocol for Health Care Professionals,'
Physical and Occupational Therapy in Geriatrics, 2
(Winter 1982), 37-51.
A written protocol for identification and assessment of
elder abuse and neglect.

Reports

178. Cooper, E. (Coordinator). *Mayor Mel Lastman's Task
Force on Abuse of the Elderly.* North York: City Hall,
1985.

The report of a task force to examine elder abuse in the city of North York, Metropolitan Toronto.

179. Cravedi, K., Modlin, M. and P. Reinecke. 'Elder Abuse: A National Disgrace: A Report.' U.S. Congress House Select Committee on Aging, Subcommittee on Health and Long Term Care, Washington, D.C., May 10, 1985.
Examines the current incidence and nature of elder abuse, assesses the extent and effectiveness of federal and state efforts to identify and prevent abuse and assist victims, and makes policy recommendations. Case histories of examples of abuse are presented, along with profiles of the elder abuser and theories on the causes of elder abuse. Responses received from a survey of state human services departments concerning their adult protective service laws, programs, and budgets are summarized, and congressional and federal action regarding elder abuse is discussed. Most states reported that elder abuse is increasing.

180. Crouse, J.S., Cobb, D.C., Harris, B.B., Kopecky, F.J. and J. Poertner. *Abuse and Neglect of the Elderly in Illinois: Incidence and Characteristics, Legislation and Policy Recommendations*. Springfield, Illinois: Sangamon State University and Illinois Department on Aging, 1981.
A study of some of the characteristics of elder abuse in Illinois.

181. D.C. Commission for Women Report. 'Suffering in Silence: A Conference on Elder Abuse' Commission for Women: Washington D.C. 1983.
The development and content of a city-wide one day conference on elder abuse held in Washington, D.C. are described, providing overall information on the topic to the general public, as well as to the elderly, caregivers, service providers, community leaders, health professionals, and the media. Prominent speakers discussed the nature and causes of elder abuse in the general session. Four workshops covered the topics of law and legal reform, caregiver problems, elder rights and responsibilities, and services for the elderly.

182. Halamandaris, V.J., 'Elder Abuse: The Hidden American Scandal,' *Caring* 5(January 1986), 16–18.

The major findings of a report on elder abuse released
by the House Select Committee on Aging are summarized.
The research and the hearings that led up to the
development of the report are described. The report
concluded that elder abuse by family members and caretakers is a full-scale national problem and that it
is increasing dramatically, despite a tendency for it
to go unreported. The report cited hundreds of typical
examples of abuse, 11 of which are summarized here. It
revealed that physical violence, including negligence,
is the most frequent type of abuse, that abuse is
likely to be repeated; that its victims are frequently
dependent women age 75 or older; and that the abuser
may very well be under considerable tension.

183. Halamandaris, V.J. 'Physical and Financial Abuse of the
     Elderly,' *Caring*, 5(January 1986), 36-7.
     Presents testimony given in September 1985 before the
     House Select Committee on Aging on the subject of
     physical and financial abuse of the elderly and on
     policy implications in the area of long term care,
     particularly home health care. Discusses problems that
     exist in the field of long term care, and lists five
     root causes of these problems, as identified by the
     Committee. Stresses the need for a national policy on
     long term care. Identifies two problems in home care
     that relate to the government's efforts to save money.
     Criticizes the methodology used to establish new limits
     on beneficiaries and providers for Medicare home health
     costs, and lists nine negative consequences that will
     result from new regulations.

184. National Clearinghouse on Family Violence. *Papers on
     Elder Abuse*. Ottawa: Health and Welfare, Canada, 1986.
     Assorted papers (mimeographed) on elder abuse can be
     obtained from this source.

185. Ontario Advisory Council on Senior Citizens. 'A Report
     on Elder Abuse,' submitted to Minister for Senior
     Citizen Affairs (January 1986).
     Report and recommendations calling for government
     measures in education, prevention and services to
     prevent elder abuse and to broaden concern to include
     institutional care facilities as well as domestic
     abuse.

186. Select Committee on Aging. 'Hearing Before the
Subcommittee on Aging House of Representatives 99th
Congress, First Session, May 10, 1985.' Washington:
U.S. Government Printing Office. (1985).
Testimony and submissions by victims and their
representatives, experts and perpetrators on the
experience of elder abuse in the home and
victimization.

187. Select Committee on Aging. *Elder Abuse: The Hidden
Problem*, U.S. House of Representatives, Comm. Pub.
pp. 96-220, Washington, D.C., U.S. Government Printing
Office, 1980. *Domestic Violence Against the Elderly*.
U.S. House of Representative, Comm. Pub. pp. 96-223,
Washington, D.C., U.S. Government Printing Office,
1980. *Elder Abuse (An Examination of a Hidden Problem)*.
U.S. House of Representatives, Comm. Pub. pp. 97-227,
Washington, D.C., U.S. Government Printing Office,
1981.
Through its survey and a review of other studies, the
House Select Committee on Aging surmises that some four
per cent of the nation's elderly may be victims of some
sort of abuse ranging from moderate to severe. Although
data was limited and mostly anecdotal, it was found
that abuse of the elderly by their families or caretakers appears to occur nation-wide and on a scale almost parallel to child abuse. The states and service
providers felt that their attempts to deal with the
problem were inadequate.

188. Shell, D. *Protection of the Elderly: A Study of Elder
Abuse*. Winnipeg, Manitoba: Manitoba Association of
Gerontology, 1982.
The author provides an exploratory study of elder abuse
in Manitoba in order to examine the nature of the problem in that province, and also to identify any possible
areas of unmet need. It is concluded that there is at
present a lack of professional awareness of the problem
and a reluctance to identify it. Suggestions are made
in terms of intervention and prevention strategies.

189. Toronto Mayor's Committee on Aging. Elder Abuse: A
Shared Problem. Toronto: City Hall, 1984.
A report of a committee dealing with elder abuse in
Toronto.

Research studies: case studies

190. Andrew, S.R. and P.A. Hall. *Alcohol Use and Elder Mistreatment: An Exploratory Study.* San Antonio, Texas, 1984 (unpublished).
Seventy-six case records were examined indicating elder mistreatment and alcohol use.

191. Dozier, C. *Report of the Elder Abuse and Neglect Assessment Instrument Field Test.* Atlanta, Georgia: The Atlanta Regional Commission, 1984 (unpublished).
An assessment instrument was tested on 52 persons in Atlanta.

192. Hageboek, J. and K. Brandt. 'Characteristics of Elderly Abuse.' Iowa: Scott County, 1981 (unpublished).
238 cases were studies to examine elder abuse.

193. Hall, P.A. and S.R. Andrew. *Minority Elder Maltreatment: Ethnicity, Gender, Age and Poverty.* San Antonio, Texas, 1984 (unpublished).
A descriptive survey of 288 abuse cases reported to the Texas Department of Human Resources in a two-year period (1982-1984).

194. Giordano, N.H. and J.A. Giordano. *Individual and Family Correlates of Elder Abuse.* Bradenton, Florida, 1984, (unpublished).
Case analysis of 600 abused and 150 non-abused elderly persons. An attempt was made to develop a profile of the abuser.

195. Phillips, L.R. 'Abuse and Neglect of the Frail Elderly at Home: An Exploration of Theometical Relationships,' *Journal of Advanced Nursing.* 8(1983), 379-92.
Sixty-three elderly persons of whom 33 were abused were interviewed. Some variables were compared in the two groups.

196. Pratt, C., Koval, J., and S. Lloyd. 'Service Workers: Responses to Abuse of the Elderly,' *Social Casework.* 64(March 1983), 147-53.
The purpose of this study was to assess service providers' and physicians' intervention responses to hypothetical cases of elder abuse. Practitioners were

asked to respond to a series of four short vignettes.
Practice and training issues relevant for the improvement of interventions and referrals in cases of elder
abuse are discussed.

197. Rounds, L.R. *A Study of Select Environmental Variables
Associated with Non-institutional Settings Where There
is Abuse or Neglect of the Elderly.* Austin, Texas:
University of Texas, 1984 (doctoral dissertation).
A case review of 45 cases active with a social agency,
to examine internal and external environments where
abuse occurs.

198. Wills, M. and J.E. Walker. 'Abuse of the Elderly: A
Preliminary Report.' Cambridge, Mass.: First National
Conference on Abuse of Older Persons, March, 1981.
Twenty-two elderly abused were interviewed for this
study.

Research studies: domestic elder abuse

199. Beachler, M.A. 'Mistreatment of Elderly Persons in the
Domestic Setting.' Texas: Brasoria County, 1979
(unpublished).
A study which attempted to document elder abuse in a
Texas county. Questionnaires were mailed to individuals
and agencies who had contact with older persons.

200. Boydston, L.S. and J.A. McNairn. 'Elder Abuse by Adult
Caretakers: An Exploratory Study.' (in) *Physical and
Financial Abuse of the Elderly.* Washington, D.C.: U.S.
House of Representatives Select Committee on Aging,
1981(April 3), 135-36. Publication no. 97-297.
Four hundred and thirty-one human service providers
received a mailed questionnaire to obtain the
prevalence of elder abuse in San Diego, California.

201. Chen, P.N., Bell, S.L., Dolinsky, D.L., Doyle, J., and
M. Dunn. 'Elderly Abuse in Domestic Settings: A Pilot
Study,' *Journal of Gerontological Social Work.* 4(Fall
1981), 3-17.
A pilot study of elder abuse in domestic settings
reveals multiple causations, symptoms, and effects, and
indicates that the public at large is unaware of and
unconcerned about the elderly victims of abuse. Current

methods and skills of intervention are inadequate and community resources are lacking for aid to both the abusers and to the abused. Recommendations for solutions and preventions of elder abuse are identified.

202. Douglass, R.L. and C. Noel. 'Domestic Abuse and Abuse of the Elderly in Michigan,' *Michigan Academician* 14(Winter 1982), 199-208.
Recent research on maltreatment of the elderly in the United States is reviewed, focusing on the major study conducted in Michigan.

203. Godkin, M.A., Wolf, R.S. and K.A. Pillemer. 'A Case Comparison Analysis of Elder Abuse and Neglect,' *International Journal of Aging and Human Development* (in press) 1987-1988 volume.
This study examines factors which contribute to elderly abuse and neglect by caregivers in a domestic setting. Methodological and conceptual variations and problems in previous studies have led to considerable confusion as to the determinants of this important social problem. A more rigorous research design was used in this study than has been previously employed. Fifty-nine abused elders from a model project site for the study of elderly abuse were compared with 49 non-abused clients from a home care program in the same agency.

204. Pillemer, K. 'The Dangers of Dependency: New Findings on Domestic Violence Against the Elderly,' *Social Problems*, 33(December 1985), 146-58.
'The elderly victims were likely to be supporting the dependent abuser.' Findings from a study of physical abuse.

205. Pillemer, K. 'Social Isolation and Elder Abuse,' *Response* 5(Fall 1985), 2-4.
From a three-year study of domestic abuse of adults over sixty years old, the author concludes that social isolation was a contributing factor. This isolation is often engineered by the abuser. Introduction of social supports such as paraprofessional aids and self-help groups are recommended.

206. Pillemer, K. *Domestic Violence Against the Elderly: A Case Control Study*. Waltham, Mass.: Brandeis

University, 1985 (doctoral dissertation, unpublished). Personal interviews with 42 abused and 42 non-abused elders.

Research studies: instruments and models

207. Fulmer, T.T. and V.M. Cahill. 'Assessing Elder Abuse: A Study,' *Journal of Gerontological Nursing* 10(December 1984), 16–20.
An instrument was developed that can be used readily by nurses to identify elderly individuals who are potential victims of physical, psychological, material, or medical abuse. The Elder Assessment Protocol (TEAP) was designed to collect data on variables that research has demonstrated to be related to symptoms of elder abuse. It was administered to all patients 70 years of age and older who came to the emergency room of the Beth Israel Hospital in Boston, Mass., during a 2-month period. The typical elderly patient was an 81-year-old woman who was mentally alert, lived at home, was on Medicare, and who came either alone or with a family member.

208. Galbraith, M.W. and R.T. Zdorkowski. 'Systemizing the Elder Abuse Research.' (in) M.W. Galbraith ed. *Convergence in Aging*, 1986, 168–76.
A critical analysis of existing research in the area of elder abuse. Research questions are posed. A model for future research is presented.

209. Hwalek, M.A. and M.C. Sengstock. 'Assessing the Probability of Abuse of the Elderly: Toward Development of a Clinical Screening Instrument,' *Journal of Applied Gerontology* 5(December 1986), 153–73.
Nine items were identified that were accurate in identifying cases into abuse/neglect categories of elder abuse.

210. Kimsey, L., Tarbox, A.R., and D.F. Bragg. 'Abuse of the Elderly – Hidden Agenda II: Future Research and Remediation,' *Journal of the American Geriatrics Society*. 29(11)1981, 503–7.
The second of two articles by these authors, this paper focuses on possible remedies for elder abuse and

suggests that the combined resources of both the legal
and medical professions and of the community-at-large
are required in order to help remedy the serious
problem.

211. King, N.R. 'Exploitation and Abuse of Older Family
     Members: An Overview of the Problem.' (in) J.J. Costa
     ed. *Abuse of the Elderly*, 1984, 3-12.
     This chapter summarizes major findings from recent
     research on elder abuse.

Research studies: large scale

212. Block, M.R. and J.D. Sinnott. *The Battered Elderly
     Syndrome: An Exploratory Study*. Maryland, College
     Park: University of Maryland, Center for Aging, 1979.
     This study attempts to obtain estimates of the
     prevalence of elder abuse.

213. Block, M. and J.D. Sinnott. The Battered Elder
     Syndrome: An Exploratory Study. Center on Aging:
     University of Maryland. 1979.
     A study on violence in American society, forms of
     family violence, elder abuse, methodology and results
     of the study, policy conclusions and a proposed
     mandatory elder abuse reporting law.

214. Crouse, J.S., Cobb, D.C., Harris, B.B., Kopecky,
     F.J. and J. Poertner. 'Abuse and Neglect of the Elderly
     in Illinois: Incidence and Characteristics, Legislation
     and Policy Recommendations.' Springfield, IL: Illinois
     Department of Aging, 1981 (unpublished).
     Nineteen hundred and eighty persons who work with older
     persons were interviewed or sent questionnaires to
     study the incidence of elder abuse in Illinois.

215. Douglass, R.I., Hickey, T., and C. Noel. *A Study of
     Maltreatment of the Elderly and Other Vulnerable
     Adults*. Ann Arbor: University of Michigan, 1980.
     A study of 228 professionals and staff in 12 nursing
     homes to determine the extent of elder abuse.

216. Elder Abuse Task Force. *Elderly Abuse in the Toledo
     Area*. Toledo, Ohio, 1984 (unpublished).

Health and social service professionals (947) and
Toledo residents (285) were surveyed to determine
incidence of abuse in Lucas County, Ohio.

217. Gioglio, G.R. *Elder Abuse in New Jersey: The Knowledge
and Experience of Abuse among Older New Jerseyans.*
Trenton, NJ: Bureau of Research, Division of Youth and
Family Services, Department of Human Services, 1983.
A sample of 387 non-institutional older persons were
investigated to obtain information on elder abuse in
New Jersey.

218. Gray Panthers of Austin. *A Survey of Abuse of the
Elderly in Texas.* Austin, Texas, 1983 (unpublished).
Fiften hundred and eight individuals and agencies were
surveyed through mailed questionnaires to find the
extent of abuse of the elderly in Texas.

219. Levenberg, J., Milan, J., Dolan, M. and P. Carpenter.
'Elder Abuse in West Virginia: Extent and Nature of the
Problem.' (in) L.G. Schultz ed. *Elder Abuse in West
Virginia: A Policy Analysis of System Response.*
Morgantown, WV: West Virginia University, 1983.
Three hundred and eighty-five individuals or agencies
were mailed questionnaires to determine the extent and
nature of abuse of the elderly.

220. McLaughlin, J.S., Nickell, J.P. and L. Gill. 'An
Epidemiological Investigation of Elder Abuse in
Southern Maine and New Hampshire.' (in) *Elder Abuse.*
Washington, D.C.: U.S. House of Representatives
Select Committee on Aging, 1980 (June 11), 111-47.
Publication No. 68-463.
Through 31 telephone interviews and 51 questionnaires
of selected professionals the authors examined elder
abuse.

221. O'Malley, H., Segars, H., Perez, R., Mitchell, V., and
G. Knuepfel. Elder Abuse in Massachusetts: A Survey of
Professionals and Paraprofessionals. Boston: Legal
Research Services for the Elderly, 1979.
An exploratory survey to provide some data on elder
abuse in Massachusetts.

222. Pennsylvania Department of Aging, Bureau of
Advocacy. 'Elder Abuse in Pennsylvania.' Harrisburg,
Pennsylvania, 1982 (unpublished).
Twenty-one hundred agencies and individuals were mailed
questionnaires in order to collect information on elder
abuse in Pennsylvania.

223. Pepper, C. and M.R. Oaker. *Elder Abuse: An Examination
of a Hidden Problem*. Washington, D.C.: U.S. Government
Printing Office, Publication No. 97-277, 1981(April 3).
Twenty states responded to a survey of incidence of
elder abuse.

224. Sengstock, M. and J. Liang. *Identifying and
Characterizing Elder Abuse*. Detroit, Michigan.
Institute of Gerontology, Wayne State University, 1982
(unpublished).
Three hundred and two social agencies were questioned
about varied aspects of elder abuse.

225. Wolf, R.S., Strugnell, C.P., and M.A. Godkin. 'Preliminary Findings from Three Model Projects on Elder
Abuse.' Worcester, Mass.: University Center on Aging,
University of Massachusetts, 1982.
Six hundred and forty-seven questionnaires were sent to
social agencies in four states to determine the nature
and extent of elder abuse.

226. Wolf, R., Godkin, M. and K. Pillemer. *Elder Abuse and
Neglect: Final Report from Three Model Projects*,
Worcester, Mass.: University of Massachusetts Medical
Center, 1984. 3 vols.
Evaluates three model projects on elder abuse which
were established in Worcester, Mass., Syracuse, N.Y.,
and Rhode Island in 1980 to demonstrate improved
mechanisms for reporting, investigating, testing, and
preventing elder abuse and neglect. Discusses the
nature and extent of elder abuse/neglect and uses
findings from two surveys of community agencies to
assess the effectiveness of education/training activities of the model projects. Case resolution, community
response, and model replicability were selected as the
criteria to measure the impact of the intervention

models. It is concluded that elder abuse/neglect cannot
be described by a single set of factors or explained by
one theory; that psychopathology is very evident in
cases of psychological abuse and to a lesser degree,
physical abuse; that there is lack of support for the
sociological factors of external stress and isolation;
and that the relationship of dependency to elder abuse/
neglect found in the gerontological literature needs to
be re-examined.

227. Wolf, R.S. 'Elder Abuse in the U.S.: Its Nature, Causes
and Some Responses,' *Ageing International*, 12(Summer
1985), 12–13.
A summary of the findings of the Massachusetts three-
year study project on elder abuse prevention and
intervention.

228. Wolf, R.S. 'Major Findings from Three Model Projects on
Elderly Abuse.' (in) K.A. Pillemer and R.S. Wolf eds.
Elder Abuse: Conflict in the Family, 1986, 218–38.
An evaluation of three model projects in Massachusetts.
What is the nature of elder abuse, its victims and
causes? What is the impact of the projects on the com-
munity?

229. Wolf, R.S., Godkin, M.A. and K.A. Pillemer. 'Maltreatment of the Elderly: A Comparative Analysis,' *Pride
Institute Journal of Long Term Home Health Care*, 5(Fall
1986), 10–17.
A short analysis of a study of 328 elder abuse cases,
which includes types of abuse, and definitions of abuse
and neglect.

Review of the literature

230. Cloke, C. 'Old Age Abuse in the Domestic Setting: A
Review.' Surrey: Age Concern England 60 Pitcairn Road,
Mitcham, Surrey, CR43LL England, 1983.
Reviews the literature on old age abuse published in
the United Kingdom and the United States. The analysis
reveals a lack of unanimity concerning the definition
of old age abuse. Likewise, knowledge about the causes
of old age abuse is sparse, primarily because much of
the research is based on a limited number of reported

cases about which few details are available. All that
can be said is that a number of factors, individually
or jointly, contribute to old age abuse, such as lack
of caregiver support, low income, poor housing, poor
family relationships, a history of family violence,
emotional stress, alcoholism, and lack of understanding
of the aging process. It is estimated that 500,000
elderly people in the United Kingdom are at risk of old
age abuse.

231. Giordano, N.H. and J.A. Giordano. 'Elder Abuse: A
Review of the Literature,' *Social Work*, 29(May/June
1984), 232-6.
This article offers an examination of the literature on
elder abuse to date in order to present a view of the
nature and the extent of the problem. Current theoretical viewpoints are outlined, and strategies for intervention are suggested.

232. Hudson, M.F. 'Elder Mistreatment: Current Research,'
(in) *Elder Abuse: Conflict in the Family*. eds.: K.A.
Pillemer and R.S. Wolf. Dover, Mass: Auburn House,
1986, 125-66.
A comprehensive review of existing research on elder
abuse in the U.S.A.

233. Hudson, M.F. and T.F. Johnson. 'Elder Neglect and
Abuse: A Review of the Literature.' (in) C. Eisdorfer
ed. *Annual Review of Gerontology and Geriatrics*. New
York: Springer, 1986. 81-133.
This review includes an analysis and summary of 31
research studies. (1979-85).

234. Steinmetz, S.K. 'Violence Between Family Members,'
Marriage and Family Review, 1(May-June 1978), 1-16.
A good review of the literature on family violence.

Social policy

235. Conley, D.M. 'Developing a Comprehensive Approach: The
Key to the Future.' (in) M.W. Galbraith ed. *Convergence
in Aging*, 1986, 177-88.
An ideal comprehensive system for coping with the
problems of elder abuse is discussed.

236. Crystal, S. 'Social Policy and Elder Abuse.' (in)
K.A. Pillemer and R.S. Wolf eds. *Elder Abuse: Conflict in the Family*, 1986, 331-40.
A discussion of needed elder abuse legislation.

237. Schultz, L.G. ed. *Elder Abuse in West Virginia: A Policy Analysis of System Response*. Morgantown, West Virginia: School of Social Work, West Virginia University, 1983.
Ten papers discuss various aspects of elder abuse in West Virginia. Topics include: definitions, extent and nature of the problem, legal interventions, the domestic violence act, the history of elder abuse, and the interdisciplinary response to elder abuse.

Special issues of journals

238. *Caring*. Vol. 5, No. 1 (January 1986). Special issue on Elder Abuse.
The lead article contains textimony from congressional hearings by a number of experts and of elder abuse victims. Articles include 'One fifth of our population at Risk' by Dr. Suzanne Steinmetz (p. 69). Other articles are: V.J. Halamandaris on 'Elder Abuse: The Hidden American Scandal' and 'Physical and Financial Abuse of the Elderly;' Lee Pearson, 'Elder Abuse: A Social Quandary;' T.O'Malley, 'Identifying and Preventing Family-Mediated Abuse and Neglect'; introduced by an editorial summary.

239. *Journal of Gerontological Nursing*. 10(December 1984): A special issue featuring various aspects of the problem of elder abuse.
Articles include Galbraith et. al. on a review of identification studies for use in self-training (21-5); Anderson et. al. on incidence and causality (6-10); an interview with elder abuse authorities Cornelia Beck and Linda Phillips on the problem of financial abuse (26-30); Floyd on data collection (11-15) and Fulmer and Cahill on a study using an elder assessment protocol (16-20).

240. *Journal of Gerontological Social Work*. 9(Spring 1986) Special issue on elder abuse.
John Poertner reports on a statewide study of elder

abuse in Illinois, utilizing a stratified random sample
(3-15); a definition of each of the three types of
elder abuse - neglect, abuse and violation of rights -
is developed by Valentine and Cash, with distinction
between social work and legal definitions. Kinderknecht
provides a guide to in-home assessment and intervention
(29-43) and Sengstock and Bennett (43-61) provide an
analysis of 30 cases of elder abuse from legal aid
files.

241. Zarit, S.N. and T. Sommers, eds. 'Caregivers,'
     Generations, 10(Fall 1985), 1-72.
     Presents 18 articles that provide an in-depth view of
     the issues faced by family caregivers and the service
     providers who seek to help them. Shows why interven-
     tions for caregivers must take individual situations
     into account. Explores the role of women in caregiving.
     Provides a familial perspective on the burden of care
     and a family systems perspective on dementia. Examines
     differences in the types of care provided by men and
     women and caregiving in minority cultures. Offers the
     stories of three family caregivers.

Surveys

242. O'Malley, H., Segars, H., Perez, R., Mitchell, V., and
     G.M. Kneupfel. 'Elder Abuse in Massachusetts: A Survey
     of Professionals and Paraprofessionals.' (in) J.J.
     Costa ed. *Abuse of the Elderly*, 1984, 57-86.
     A survey conducted during the period of October 1977
     through March 1979. The major findings are presented.

243. Sengstock, M.C., Barrett, S. and R. Graham. 'Abused
     Elders: Victims of Villains or of Circumstances?'
     Journal of Gerontological Social Work, 8(Fall/Winter
     1984), 101-11.
     A study of survey data on a number of social, psycho-
     logical and concrete factors in families where elder
     abuse occurs. Authors recommend a three-pronged ap-
     proach of protection for victims, service to abuser
     and reduction of environmental stresses.

244. Zdorkowski, R.T. and M.G. Galbraith. 'An Inductive
     Approach to the Investigation of Elder Abuse,' *Ageing
     and Society*, 5(December 1985), 413-29.

The findings of the elder abuse surveys conducted in
the United States are not strictly comparable, although
they may be combined to suggest a more organised approach to elder abuse research. This paper presents a
model of elder abuse derived from those studies, and
suggests that abuse is the predictable outcome of the
interactions between and among elders' and abusers'
characteristics. A list of the research hypotheses
suggested by the model is presented, two forms of
analysis that could be used to test them are described,
and the implications of this model for scholars and
practitioners are outlined.

Theoretical aspects

245. Ansello, E.F., King, N.R. and G. Taler. 'The Environ-
     mental Press Model: A Theoretical Framework For Inter-
     vention in Elder Abuse.' (in) K.A. Pillemer and R.S.
     Wolf eds. *Elder Abuse: Conflict in the Family*, 1986,
     314-30.
     A theoretical model for comprehensive intervention in
     elder abuse. The model is based on established social
     theory.

246. Gelles, R.J. and M.A. Straus. 'Determinants of Violence
     in the Family: Toward a Theoretical Integration.' (in)
     Contemporary Theories About the Family, vol. 1 edited
     by W.R. Burr et. al. New York: The Free Press, 1979,
     549-81.
     A thorough discussion of the various theories under-
     lying the topic of family violence.

247. Phillips, L.R. 'Theoretical Explanations of Elder
     Abuse: Competing Hypotheses and Unresolved Issues.'
     (in) K.A. Pillemer and R.S. Wolf eds. *Elder Abuse:
     Conflict in the Family*, 1986, 197-217.
     Explores three competing theories that have been
     advanced to explain elder abuse: the situational model,
     social exchange theory and symbolic interactionism.

Treatment issues

248. Beth Israel Hospital Elder Assessment Team. 'An Elder
     Abuse Assessment Team in an Acute Hospital
     Setting,' *The Gerontologist*, 26(April 1986), 115-18.

Response to public concerns regarding elder abuse and neglect has resulted in mandatory 'elder abuse reporting laws' in many states. This paper describes a hospital-based multidisciplinary team at Boston's Beth Israel Hospital, designed to assess and respond to cases of suspected abuse or neglect of elders from both institutional and community settings. Presence of the team has increased the hospital staff's awareness of elder abuse and neglect, as well as their willingness to refer suspected cases for further assessment.

249. Carr, K. et. al. 'An Elder Abuse Assessment Team in an Acute Hospital Setting,' *Gerontologist*, 26(April 1986), 115-18.
This paper describes the Beth Israel Hospital Elder Assessment Team, a multi-disciplinary group designed to assess and respond to cases of suspected abuse or neglect of elders from institution and community. Program was found to raise awareness and referrals.

250. Davis, L.J. and E.M. Brody. *Rape and Older Women: A Guide to Prevention and Protection*. Rockville, Maryland: National Institute of Mental Health, 1979.
The authors outline educational and training tools for older women, community groups, and social agencies.

251. Edinberg, M.A. 'Developing and Integrating Family-Oriented Approaches in Care of the Elderly,' (in) K.A. Pillemer and R.S. Wolf eds. *Elder Abuse: Conflict in the Family*, 1986, 267-82.
An outline of several aspects of what can be termed a 'family-oriented approach' to the care of the elderly.

252. Goldmeier, J. 'Helping the Elderly in Times of Stress,' *Social Casework*, 66(June 1985), 323-32.
For intervention to be sensitive to elderly clients, it should be designed as part of a larger treatment plan. Treatment of the elderly is discussed as a continuing process in which the stresses of aging - abuse and exploitation, relocation, and the like - are taken into account. A framework for time-limited, ongoing intervention with this population is proposed, the prominent stresses of aging are inventoried, and suggestions for the timing of interventions in various stressful situations are offered.

253. Kinney, M.B., Wendt, R. and J. Hurst. 'Elder
     Abuse: Techniques for Effective Resolution.' (in)
     M.W. Galbraith ed. *Convergence in Aging*, 1986.
     Issues in responding to elder abuse are discussed in
     this chapter. Treatment modalities are also included.

254. Lau, E.E. 'Inpatient Geropsychiatry in the Network of
     Elder Abuse Services.' (in) M.W. Galbraith ed.
     Convergence in Aging, 1986, 65-80.
     A description of the work at the Lutheran Medical
     Center in Cleveland, Ohio. The clinical team in the
     Geropsychiatry Unit reports that 10 per cent of the
     patients are suffering from some type of abuse.

255. Myers, J.E. and B. Sheldon. 'Abuse and the Older
     Person: Issues and Implications for Counselors,'
     Journal of Counseling and Development, 65(7), 1987,
     376-80.
     A discussion of how counselors can deal with abuse of
     the elderly.

256. Rathbone-McCuan, E. and R.K. Goodstein. 'Elder Abuse:
     Clinical Considerations,' *Psychiatric Annals*, 15(May
     1985), 331-33.
     Discusses clinical considerations in the identification
     and treatment of victims of elder abuse. The common
     denominator of abused elderly persons is that their
     disabilities cause them to be dependent on and burden-
     some to the family or paid caregiver. Abuse of the
     elderly encompasses physical, verbal, and psychological
     abuse; misuse of property and money; theft and/or ex-
     ploitation of belongings; and the denial of fundamental
     resources and health care. Clinicians frequently fail
     to perceive abuse of the elderly or deny it exists.
     Elderly victims often exhibit a self imposed silence
     due to apathy or fear of retaliation. It is difficult
     to verify instances of abuse and assess intentionality.

257. Rathbone-McCuan, E., Travis, A. and B. Voyles. 'Family
     Intervention: The Task Centered Approach.' (in)
     J. Kosberg ed. *Abuse and the Maltreatment of the
     Elderly*, 1983, 355-75.
     The task-centered model appears to be helpful to the
     aged client and to significant others.

Volunteers

258. Zdorkowski, R.T. 'Older Volunteers and Their Potential
    for Identifying and Treating Elder Abuse.' (in)
    M.W. Galbraith ed. *Convergence in Aging*, 1986, 81–94.
    A survey of volunteers who work with the homebound
    elderly, and their abilities to detect abuse.

Women and elder abuse

259. Block, M.R. 'Special Problems and Vulnerability of
    Elderly Women.' (in) J. Kolsberg ed. *Abuse and
    Maltreatment of the Elderly*, 1983, 220–33.
    Elderly women are more vulnerable to certain types
    of crime and victimization than elderly men, particu-
    larly rape, purse snatching, elder abuse, burglary and
    fraud.

260. Cohen, L. *Small Expectations: Society's Betrayal of
    Older Women*. Toronto: McClelland and Stewart, 1984.
    Explores society's treatment of women as they age.
    Self-image, health, housing, violence, poverty, etc.

261. Cohen, L. 'Violence Against Older Women: An Inter-
    national Survey.' An unpublished report produced for
    the Canadian Advisory Council on the Status of Women,
    Oct. 1982. Available from: CACSW, Box 1541, Station B,
    Ottawa, K1P 5R5.
    The purpose of this survey was to assess what is being
    done on the international level as far as violence
    against older women is concerned, and to ultimately
    explore possible creative responses to the problem in a
    number of different jurisdictions. Britain, the U.S.,
    Israel, Holland and France were chosen for study.

262. Hooyman, N.R. and S. Fallcreek. 'Older Women as Victims
    of Violence,' (in) A. Weick and S.T. Vandiver eds.
    Women, Power and Change. Washington, D.C., National
    Association of Social Workers Inc., 1982. pp. 49–64.
    This article illustrates how society's devaluation of
    older persons (especially older women) encourages
    acceptance of violence as understandable, unavoidable,
    or even deserved. Two types of violence are focussed
    upon: abuse inflicted by familial caretakers, and

sexual assault by nonfamily members. Implications for
service providers are discussed.

263. Schlesinger, R.A. 'Granny-Bashing: An Introduction to
the Problem,' *Canadian Woman Studies*. 5(Spring 1984),
56-9.
This article briefly examines how women are affected by
the problems of elder abuse. General profiles of the
abusers and of the abused are presented, and the question of why elder abuse occurs is asked. Suggestions
are offered for practitioners.

Late entries

264. Clark, D.M. 'Elder Abuse.' (in) *Psychogeriatrics: A
Practical Handbook*, ed. by Darleen Retozinsky,
Toronto: Gage Educational Publishing, 1987, 173-82.
An overview of elder abuse which includes definition,
types of abuse, theories of causation and intervention.

265. Moore, T. and V. Thompson. 'Elder Abuse: A Review of
Research, Programmes and Policy,' *The Social Worker*,
55(Fall 1987), 115-22.
This paper reviews Canadian and American research
regarding elder abuse. The gaps in the legal and policy
area are identified in the Canadian setting.

266. Sengstock, M.C. and M. Hwalek. 'A Review and Analysis
of Measures for the Identification of Elder Abuse,'
Journal of Gerontological Social Work, 10(3-4) 1987,
21-36.
This study examined seven elder abuse identification
measures. Recommendations are made for improving
methods of identifying elderly victims of abuse.

267. Senior Citizens Secretariat, Nova Scotia. *Elder Abuse:
Everyone's Concern*. Halifax, Nova Scotia, 1986 (P.O.
Box 2065, Halifax, N.S. B3J 2Z1).
A summary of the present knowledge about abuse of the
elderly. Contains the new legal act to provide protec-
tion of adults from abuse and neglect (Bill No. 61).

RESOURCES

Research studies completed on abuse of the elderly
(1979-1985)

1979
Beachler
    208 individuals
Block and Sinnott
    427 professionals,
    443 elderly persons
Lau and Kosberg*
    404 cases
O'Malley et al. 1979
    1,004 professionals/
    paraprofessionals

1980
Douglass, Hickey and Noel
    228 professionals
McLaughlin, Nickell and Gill
    31 telephone interviews,
    51 questionnaires
Steuer and Austin
    12 abused elderly persons

1981
Boydstone and McNairn
    431 professionals
Chen et al.*
    90 professionals
Crouse et al
    1,980 persons who work
    with elderly

Hageboeck and Brandt
    238 cases
Pepper and Oakar*
    questionnaires to 50
    states
Wills and Walker
    22 elderly abused persons

1982
Pennsylvania Dept. of Aging
    2,100 agencies and persons
Sengstock and Liang
    302 agencies
Wolf, Strugnell and Godkin
    647 questiionnaires to 4
    states (social agencies)
1983
Gioglo and Blakemore
    387 elderly persons
Gray Panthers of Austin
    1,508 agencies and persons
Levenberg et al.
    385 persons and agencies
Phillips*
    63 elderly persons (33
    abused)
Pratt, Koval and Lloyd*
    350 social workers 250
    physicians

Steinmetz*
   77 adult caretakers

1984
Andrew and Hall
   76 cases of abuse
Dozier
   52 elderly persons
Elderly Abuse Task Force
   947 professionals, 285
   public persons
Giordano and Giordano
   600 abused and 150
   non-abused cases
Hall and Andrew
   288 abused cases

O'Brien, Hudson and Johnson
   3,001 health care
   providers
Rounds
   45 cases of abuse

1985
Phillips and Rempusheski*
   29 social workers and
   nurses
Pillemer
   42 abused, 42 non-abused
   elders

1. The bibliographic notations on all the studies can be found in the Annotated Bibliography under *Research Studies*.

2. For complete descriptions and analysis of the studies see: Hudson, M.F. and T.J. Johnson, 'Elder Neglect and Abuse: A Review of the Literature.' (in) C. Eisdorfer, ed. *Annual Review of Gerontology and Geriatrics*. New York: Springer, 1986, 81-133.

3. The studies marked with an asterisk are published, the rest are unpublished.

A basic library on abuse of the elderly

1. Anetzberger, G.J. *The Etiology of Elder Abuse by Adult Offspring*. Springfield, Ill.: Charles C. Thomas, 1987.
2. Brillon, Y. *Victimization and Fear of Crime Among the Elderly*. Toronto: Butterworths 1987.
3. Costa, J.J. *Abuse of the Elderly*. Lexington, Mass.: D.C. Heath, 1984.
4. Galbraith, M.W. ed. *Elder Abuse: Perspectives on an Emerging Crisis*. Convergence in Aging, Kansas: Mid-America Congress on Aging, 1986.
5. Johnston, T.F., O'Brien, J.E. and M.F. Hudson. *Elder Neglect and Abuse: An Annotated Bibliography*. Westport, Conn.: Greenwood Press, 1985.
6. Kosberg, J.I. (ed.) *Abuse and Maltreatment of the Elderly: Causes and Interventions*. Boston: John Wright, 1983.
7. Pillemer, K.A. and R.S. Wolf (eds.) *Elder Abuse: Conflict in the Family*. Dover, Mass.: Auburn House, 1986.
8. Quinn, M.J. and S.K. Tomita. *Elder Abuse and Neglect: Causation, Diagnosis, and Intervention Strategies*. New York: Springer, 1986.
9. Yin, P. *Victimization and the Aged*. Springfield, Ill.: Charles C. Thomas, 1985.

Addresses of publishers

Auburn House Publishing Co., 14 Dedham St., Dover, Mass. 02030-0658
Butterworths, 2265 Midland Ave. Scarborough, Ont. M1P 4S1
Greenwood Press, 80 Post Rd. W., P.O. Box 5007, Westport, Conn. 02173
Heath Publishing, Lexington Books, 125 Spring St., Lexington, Mass. 02173
Mid-America Congress on Aging: 9400 State Ave., Room 111, Kansas City, Kansas 66112
Springer Publishing, 536 Broadway, New York, NY 10012
Charles C. Thomas, 2600 First St., Springfield, IL 62794-9265
John Wright, 5 Great Road, Littleton, Mass. 01460

Visual aids

1. Department of Social and Rehabilitation Services, State
   of Montana, P.O. Box 4210, Helena, MT 59604
   (406) 444-3865
   Elder Abuse: Everyone's Concern
   Dramatization of an unintentional elder abuse situation
   from beginning stressors through typical response from a
   social service agency. Created for public awareness
   purposes and to encourage people to report.
   1984   30-minute videotape(C)
   Purchase price: $20 1/2"; rental: no charge

2. Family and Child Abuse Prevention Center, 1 Stranahan
   Square, Ste. 134, Toledo, OH 43604 (419) 244-3054
   Elder Abuse: The Invisible Problem
   General overview of abuse/neglect, its scope, causes,
   and interventions. For community audiences. Production
   staged.
   1986   15-minute slide/tape(C)
   Purchase price: $95

3. SPEC Associates, 15344 Artesian, Detroit, MI 48223
   (313) 272-4853
   Identify the Victim
   Staged slides intended to help identify six types of
   abused and neglect. Designed for use with the *Sengstock-
   Hwalek Comprehensive Index of Elder Abuse*.
   1986   24-minute slide/tape, videotape(C)
   Purchase price: $100 prepaid slide/tape, 1/2", 3/4"
   (P.O. or invoice add $18 handling)

4. Department of Social Work, Hampden University, Hampden,
   VA 23668 (804) 727-5587
   Identifying and Reporting Elder Abuse
   Three simulated incidents illustrating physical, psychological, and material abuse. Definitions of each type of
   abuse and intervention strategies appropriate to
   Virginia legislation explained.Four short pamphlet sup-
   plements.
   1985   30-minute videotape(C)
   Purchase price: $125 3/4"; $95 1/2" (price includes 100
   pamphlets in multiples of 25. For videotape only, deduct
   $30)

5. Michigan Department of Social Services, 300 S. Capitol
   Street, Ste. 707, Lansing, MI 48909 (517) 373–9170
   *Protecting Adults in Michigan: Rights, Responsibilities
   and Realities*
   Adult protective services workers' perspectives on a
   wide range of dramatized incidents which portray elder
   abuse situations and interventions. The laws represent
   Michigan but apply to other states as well. Used for
   training. Updated on Michigan legislation added to film
   in 1983.
   1980   30-minute film(C)
   Purchase price: $150 16 mm; rental: no charge

6. Films Incorporated, 5547 N. Ravenswood Ave., Chicago, IL
   60640–1199 (800) 323–4222, (312) 878–7300
   Ready or Not, Here I Come
   Issues raised through actual case history interviews
   with victims, perpetrators, and authorities. Several
   types of abuse/neglect depicted. Domestic and nursing
   home abuse represented. Discussion of issues during last
   half of presentation. Production by John Weiskopf.
   1985   52-minute film, videotape(C)
   Purchase price: $198 1/2"; $298 3/4"; rental: $90

7. Kinetic Film Enterprises Ltd., 255 Delaware Avenue,
   Ste. 340, Buffalo, NY 14202 (716) 856–7631
   In Canada: Mobius International, 188 Davenport Rd.,
   Toronto, Ont. (416) 964–8484
   The Silence Upstairs
   Case study dramatization of one family's experience when
   three generations live under one roof. Caregiver burden
   in this situation is presented.
   1985   13-minute film, videotape(C)
   Purchase price: $296 16 mm, 1/2" (free preview for
   purchase); rental: available

8. Media Services Division, M.C. 151-E, Texas Dept. of
   Human Resources, P.O. Box 2960, Austin, TX 78769
   (512) 450–4251, 450–4247
   A Time to Mourn
   Realistic slides geared to incidence and intervention
   in Texas, identifies types of abuse/neglect and some
   causes. Encourages public awareness and hot line
   reporting. Mentions ethical considerations briefly.
   1983   13-minute slide/tape(C)
   Purchase price: $50

9. Films Incorporated, 5547 N. Ravenswood Avenue, Chicago, IL 60640–1199 (800) 323–4222, (312) 878–7300
   The Wild Goose
   Satirizes nursing home life and care. Limited use, perhaps in educational settings to discuss such issues as stereotyping, infantilizing.
   1973   18-minute film, videotape(B/W)
   Purchase price: $129 1/2"; $198 3/4"; $375 16 mm

10. University Media Services, California State University, Sacto, 6000 Jay Street, Sacramento, CA 95819 (916) 278–5763 (purchase), 278–5760 (rental)
    Suffering in Silence: Abuse of the Elderly
    Overview of elder abuse problem using actual case history and interviews with direct service providers, medical personnel, and criminal justice staff. Various intervention options discussed. Cultural values and their impact presented.
    1985   30-minute videotape(C)
    Purchase price: $250 + 6% tax 3/4"; rental: $35 3/4"

11. Project Idea, University Center on Aging, University of Massachusetts Medical Center, 55 Lake Ave. North, Worcester, MA 01605–2397
    Elder Abuse and Neglect in the Family series.
    'The Hidden Sorrow: An Overview'
    Examination of definitions of 'abuse' and 'neglect,' causes and manifestations of abuse through conversations with actual victims, medical staff, and elder abuse professionals.
    'In Pursuit of a Life Without Violence: Intervention Strategies' (24 min)
    Discussion of four actual cases of elder abuse: conducting an assessment, developing a service plan, coordinating community services, using the legal system, and building trusting relationships. (26 min)
    'Difficult Choices: Ethical Issues in Casework'
    Examination of one elder abuse case by a caseworker, lawyers, and elder abuse professionals. Issues of competence, the reluctant victim, and quality of life are raised. (20 min)
    Purchase price: $75 per videotape; $180 for series; rental: $25 per videotape; $60 for series

12. Rape Crisis Network, North 1226 Howard Street, Spokane, WA 99201 (509) 624–7273

Age Makes no Difference
An 87-year-old woman tells the story of her own rape,
gives suggestions for self-protection, and explains how
she regained control over her own life after the
assault. A convicted rapist speaks about rape from
behind prison walls, discussed various motives for com-
mitting rape, and offers ways that a victim can respond
in a threatening situation.
n.d.   13-minute 16 mm(C)
Purchase price: $250 16 mm; rental: $20

13. Gerontology Institute of New Jersey, P.O. Box 345,
    Milltown, NJ 08850
    Elder Abuse - A Plan for Action
    Tape 1: 'Patricia Moore, Author, Disguised - A True
    Story. Law Enforcement's Response to the Elderly.'
    Examination of research and responses to elder abuse in
    the United States.
    Tape 2: 'Service Delivery for the Frail Elderly.' Expo-
    sition of intervention strategies, ecological approach
    for diagnosis, interdisciplinary team planning, com-
    munity neglect, case management, legal procedures, and
    impact of present social and health policies on the
    frail elderly.
    Tape 3: 'Panel Implementing Recommendations to Eliminate
    Elder Abuse.' Discussion of respite services, dynamics
    of domestic violence prevention and control, and imple-
    menting respite programs and policies.
    Purchase price: $65.00 videotape/VHS (plus shipping)

Addresses of selected sources cited in bibliography

American Public Welfare Association, 1125 Fifteenth St. N.W. Washington, DC 20005

Annual Review of Gerontology and Geriatrics, Springer Publishing, 536 Broadway, New York, NY 10012-3955

Auburn House Publishing, 14 Dedham St., Dover, MA 02030-0658

Ageing and Society, Cambridge University Press, 32 East 57th St., New York, NY 10022

Butterworths, 2265 Midland Ave., Scarborough, Ont. M1P 4S1

Consortium for Elder Abuse Prevention, Mount Zion Hospital and Medical Center, P.O. Box 7921, San Francisco, CA 94120

Convergence in Aging, Mid-America Congress on Aging, 9400 State Ave., Room 111, Kansas City, KS 66112

J.W. Crane Memorial Library, Canadian Geriatrics Research Society, 351 Christie St., 2nd Floor, Toronto, Ont. M6G 3C3

C.A.N.E. Exchange, College of Human Sources, University of Delaware, Newark, Delaware 19716
   A clearinghous on elder abuse and neglect. Publishes a
   bulletin. Conducts informal searches and provides at
   cost, copies of materials in the clearinghouse archives.

Daedalus, P.O. Box 515, Canton, MA 02021

Elder Abuse Report, Project IDEA, University Center on Aging, University of Massachusetts Medical Center, 55 Lake Ave. North, Worcester, MA 01605-2397

Family Relations, National Council on Family Relations, 1910 West County Road B, Ste. 147, Saint Paul, MN 55113

Family Research Laboratory, 128 Horton Social Science Center, University of New Hampshire, Durham, NH 03824-3586

Family Violence Bulletin, Psychology Department, University of Texas at Tyler, 3900 University Blvd., Tyler, TX 75701

Family Violence Research Program, University of Texas, at Tyler, Department of Psychology, 3900 University Blvd., Tyler, TX 75701

Geriatric Medicine, Druid Publishing, 52 St. Clair Ave. E., Toronto, Ont. M4T 1M9

The Gerontology Research Centre, Simon Fraser University, Burnaby, B.C. V5A 1S6

Greenwood Press, 88 Post Rd. W., P.O. Box 5007, Westport, CT 06881

Health and Social Work, National Association of Social Workers, 257 Park Ave. South, New York, NY 10010

Journal of Applied Gerontology, Sage Publications, 2111 West Hillcrest Drive, Newbury Park, CA 91320

Journal of Family Violence, Plenum Publishing, 233 Spring St., New York, NY 10013

Journal of Gerontological Social Work, Haworth Press, 28 East 22nd St., New York, NY 10010-6110

Journal of Interpersonal Violence, Sage Publications, 275 South Beverly Dr., Beverly Hills, CA 90212

Lexington Books, C.D. Heath, Ste. 1600, 100 Adelaide St. W., Toronto, ont. M5H 1S9

Manitoba Council on Aging, 7th Floor, 175 Hargrave St., Winnipeg, Man. R3C 3R8

Mayor Mel Lastman's Task Force on Abuse of the Elderly, North York City Hall, 5100 Yonge St., North York, Ont. M2N 5V7

Mid-America Congress on Aging, 9400 State Ave., Room 111, Kansas City, KS 66112

National Clearinghouse on Family Violence, Dept. of National Health and Welfare, Brooke Claxton Building, Ottawa, Ont. K1A 1B5

National Institute of Mental Health, 5600 Fishers Lane, Rockville, MD 20857

Programme in Gerontology, University of Toronto, 455 Spadina Ave., Room 406, Toronto, Ont. M5S 1A1

Project Share, National Clearinghouse for Improving the Management of Human Services, P.O. Box 2309, Rockville, MD 20852

Social Casework, 44 E. 23rd St., New York, NY 10010

Solicitor General of Canada, 340 Laurier Ave. W., Ottawa, Ont. K1A OP8 (Communications Group)

Social Work, National Association of Social Workers, 257 Park Ave. South, New York, NY 10010

Task Force on Family Violence Northumberland County. Robert A. Kerr, Coordinator, Family and Children's Services of Northumberland, 230 Walton St., Port Hope, Ont. L1A 1P2

Task Force on Prevention of Elder Abuse, Social Planning and Research Council of British Columbia, 106, 2182 West 12th Ave., Vancouver, B.C. V6K 2N4

Charles C. Thomas Publishers, 2600 South First St., Springfield, IL 62717

Toronto Mayor's Committee on Aging, City Clerk, City Hall, Toronto, ont. M5H 2N2

Vanier Institute of the Family, Resource and Information Centre, 120 Holland Ave., Ottawa, Ont. K1Y OX6

Violence and Victims, Springer Publishing, 536 Broadway, New York, NY 10012

Vis à Vis, Newsletter, Family Violence Program, Canadian Council on Social Development, P.O. Box 3505, Station C, 55 Parkdale Ave., Ottawa, Ont. K1Y 4G1

West Virginia University, School of Social Work, Morgantown, WV 26506

AUTHOR INDEX

Ambrogi, D. 120
American Public Welfare
  Association 121
Amsden, D.J. 45
Anderson, C.L. 152
Anderson, L. 54, 132
Andrew, S.R. 193
Andrew, W.R. 190
Anetzberger, G.J. 30
Ansello, E.F. 245
Astrein, B. 115
Austin, E. 167

Bahr, R.T. 153
Barrett, S. 243
Beachler, M.A. 199
Beck, C.M. 4, 38, 39, 96
Bell, S.L. 201
Bengtson, V. 7
Beth Israel Hospital Elder
  Elder Assessment Team
  248
Blank, A. 142
Block, M.R. 212, 213, 259
Bookin, D. 157
Boydston, L.S. 200
Bragg, D.F. 144, 168, 210
Brandt, K. 192
Brillon, Y. 57
Brody, E.M. 250
Brown, J.A. 88
Brubaker, T.H. 8

Cahill, V.M. 207
Callahan, J.J. 138
Campion, E. 102
Canadian Association of
  Social Work Administrators
  in Health Facilities 89
Canadian Journal on Aging 9
Caring 238
Caro, F.G. 40
Carpenter, P. 219
Carr, K. 249
Carrière, R. 18
Cazenave, N.A. 78
Center, L.J. 62
Champlin, L. 107
Chappell, N. 11
Chen, P.N. 201
Cicirelli, V.G. 41
Clark, D.M. 264
Clarke, A.H. 58
Clemente, F. 59
Cloke, C. 230
Cobb, D.C. 161, 180, 214
Cohen, L. 260, 261
Conley, D.M. 235
Cooper, E. 178
Cornell, C.P. 91
Costa, J.J. 1, 2, 19, 31,
  76, 179
Cravedi, K. 179
Crouse, J.S. 180, 214
Crystal, S. 236

Rachel Schlesinger

Rachel Aber Schlesinger obtained her B.Sc. and M.A. degrees
from Cornell University, School of Human Ecology. She
majored in Child Development and Family Relations. Her
Doctorate in Education was granted by the University of
Toronto, O.I.S.E., department of adult education. In addition to university degrees, Dr Schlesinger has teaching
qualifications for the State of New York, U.S.A., the
Province of Ontario, and New Zealand.

An interest in ethnicity and multiculturalism was
fueled for Dr Schlesinger by her experience in living and
working in various countries, such as India (where she ran
a nursery school), Australia (where she taught at the
Kindergarten college), New Zealand (working as a consultant
to the Ministry of Education and teaching school) and
Jamaica (working for the Jamaica Children's Aid, in
cross-country adoptions).

A need to understand how we can effect social and
individual change led Rachel to her doctoral research
dealing with issues of how women understand transitions
and changes in their lives. This led to further research in
working with groups of women, banding together into support
networks as they returned to the full-time workforce. Her
ongoing interest in how women communicate and how communication in groups can facilitate change led to projects dealing
with violence and abuse of women of all ages. It is necessary to establish information, to find ways to help women
who are being abused, and to devise prevention programs.
These various aspects have led Dr Schlesinger to research,
and produce training manuals for use in groups. In addition,
she is involved with studies that are carried out dealing

with changes in marriage, child-bearing and rearing,
and health issues.

At present, Rachel Schlesinger teaches at York University, Toronto, in Social Science and in the Faculty of
Education. In addition to teaching, writing and researching,
she is involved on the national board of Hadassah-WIZO, is
married to Ben, has four children, and two daughters-in-law.

Benjamin Schlesinger

Ben Schlesinger was born in Berlin, Germany in 1928. After
living in Belgium, France, and Portugal, he arrived as a
refugee in Canada in 1942. He received his B.A. (Sociology)
from Sir George Williams College in Montreal in 1951,
his M.S.W. from the University of Toronto (Social Work) in
1953, and his Ph.D. from Cornell University in 1961 (Family
Relationships). He also was an intern in psychotherapy in
Detroit (1957-8). He worked for 8 years as a social worker
with families and children.

Dr Schlesinger has been on the staff of the Faculty of
Social Work at the University of Toronto since 1960. Presently he is a Professor, with special interests related to
the Canadian Family.

He is author and editor of nineteen books: *The Multi-
Problem Family*, 3rd ed., *Poverty in Canada and the U.S.A.*,
The One Parent Family, 4th ed., *The Jewish Family*, *Family
Planning in Canada: A Source Book*, *Sexual Behaviour in
Canada*, *Sexual Abuse of Children: A Resource Guide and
Annotated Bibliography*, *The One-Parent Family in the 1980's*,
and *Sexual Abuse of Children in the 1980's*, all published
by the University of Toronto Press. A Japanese version of
the *One-Parent Family in the 1980's* was published in
1987. The book *Families: A Canadian Persepective, and
Families: Canada* (also *Familles: Canada*) was published by
McGraw-Hill Ryerson, *The Chatelaine Guide to Marriage* by
MacMillan, and *One in Ten: The Single Parent in Canada*, by
the Guidance Centre, Faculty of Education, University of
Toronto. *Jewish Family Issues* (Garland Press) was published
in 1987.

Dr Schlesinger has a keen interest in international
social work and welcomed the opportunity of joining the
Faculty of 'Aloka' the Advanced Study and Training Centre
in Yelwal, Mysore, India (1959-60). The 'Aloka' Centre,

sponsored by the World Assembly in Youth, provided leader-
ship training for young Asian and African leaders. During
the academic year 1966–67, he was Visiting Professor of
Social Work at the University of West Indies in Jamaica
under the Canadian External Aid Programme. During the 1971–
72 academic year he was Visiting Lecturer at the University
of Western Australia in Perth, Australia, in the Department
of Social Work. During the 1978–79 academic year he was
Visiting Professor, Department of Sociology, University of
Auckland, New Zealand.

He is the general editor of the 'Social Problems in
Canada' series and the ''Canadian Social Patterns' series
published by the Guidance Centre, Faculty of Education,
University of Toronto. He is the author of six booklets in
these series. He is married to Rachel, and they have four
children.